PINEAL GLAND

The Step by Step Guide to Open Your Chakras and
the Third Eye

(Increase Your Awareness and Consciousness.
Chakra and Foresight!)

Bryan Hairston

Published by Kevin Dennis

Bryan Hairston

All Rights Reserved

Pineal Gland: The Step by Step Guide to Open Your Chakras and the Third Eye (Increase Your Awareness and Consciousness. Chakra and Foresight!)

ISBN 978-1-989965-53-5

Legal & Disclaimer

The information contained in this book is not designed to replace or take the place of any form of medicine or professional medical advice. The information in this book has been provided for educational and entertainment purposes only.

The information contained in this book has been compiled from sources deemed reliable, and it is accurate to the best of the Author's knowledge; however, the Author cannot guarantee its accuracy and validity and cannot be held liable for any errors or omissions. Changes are periodically made to this book. You must consult your doctor or get professional medical advice before using any of the suggested remedies, techniques, or information in this book.

Table of Contents

Introduction

This book contains proven steps and strategies on how to become better at being a sensitive and highly accurate psychic. There are plenty of methods to unlocking this power and in this book, we tackle some of the most effective ones.

Here's an inescapable fact: Having psychic abilities will definitely come in handy at some point—there are certain situations in life when you might need to know or better understand something, but have no access to essential information. Think of the times when certain knowledge was hidden from you and how that affected your decision making. To avoid future incidents like that, developing and harnessing your psychic abilities is of great importance.

Being psychic isn't just about predicting future events. Most of the time, it can really help you deal with the present. It allows you to foresee the consequences of certain decisions, whether they may be the ones you make or those made by people around you.

Gaining a better understanding of this skill means you would no longer need to rely on ordinary means of acquiring information, but instead taps to a source of info that transcends the limitations of time and space. This, alone, gives you a significant advantage over other people who tend to only see things through one perspective—the present.

All of us humans are born with a "third eye" but the majority are not aware that they even have one. Some, simply don't believe in it. It is a common misconception to think that only special people are born with this gift. The fact is, some people are more conscious of their psychic abilities and they do not dismiss it as mere coincidence or fantasy. Others are born highly sensitive and notice their ability even at a very young age.

Whether you want to further increase your abilities or want to start developing them, the key to making this happen is constant practice. In this book, we'll show you exactly how you can do that.

Please use what you learn wisely. We wish you the best of luck!

Chapter 1: What Is the Third Eye?

The third eye enables people to see what most people can't. It is being able to see potential. All people have access to their third eye. For instance, when you have an intuition and act in response to it, you are actually using your third eye. However, that is just the tip of what your third eye can actually do. Your third eye is actually an undeveloped sense, and once you develop and refine it, you can see more accurately, more than just intuitions.

The third eye is a part of each individual. You can think of it as an organ that integrates your mind and your senses so they can work together and make a powerful set of sensory organs. The third eye can undergo a natural evolution which allows a person to see more patterns in life. More than that, it can show you hidden patterns by overlaying these over your other senses.

Being the sixth sense, the third eye can be used in many ways possible. Most seers use the third eye to understand patterns and answer different questions. They feel some sort of energy playing around then and they consciously take control of this energy. For instance, when you empathize with another, you are using your third eye to put yourself on the shoes of others and feel their emotions.

See Through the Sixth Sense

The third eye works in a different way. To understand this better, take the example of sensing and interpreting energy. We see motion such as in a moving vehicle, we see activity as we drive the vehicle, and sense an exchange of energy with the gas burning from driving. We are also able to sense and project the potential by predicting where the vehicle is directed based on where the roads lead. This way, we are seeing motion, activities, and exchange of energies that flow simultaneously. When you integrate these altogether, you can have a visual map that sees energy play out. You see the energy as an overlay instead of an abstract concept and it is when it turns into a concrete concept in life. It becomes a tangible property that we can sense more deeply.

But this idea is rebuttable. Can we actually see energy? Of course, not directly. Whereas our eyes could see the results of the interaction of energies, directly seeing the energy is a different thing. Our eyes just see what they are designed to see — the visible light. What the third eye can do is process the information and make it an overlay of other senses, enabling us to sense and interpret energies more accurately. Through this, we can have a deeper understanding of the energies that we "see".

When you think about it, this idea actually makes sense. Our minds are able to figure out something and tell us what it is all about. And these ideas are formed through the integration of our five senses. This may sound like a mystical power being able to use our sixth sense and see or predict the potential which is not apparent at the moment, but this is a tangible skill which people can acquire.

There may be a lot of misinterpretations and mistranslations because we depend so much on our ability to interpret different results. The facts that we see may be different from the information that our third eye brings to us. And because most of us see things in a different way, sharing to others what the third eye sees may be problematic. For instance, when we hear the word glass, we may make different visual interpretations of glasses because what one person sees may be different from others. The ability to see the world in different angles is unique to us. However, commonalities still occur because we are zeroed and grounded towards common baselines for coherence.

It is, therefore, not so surprising how we differ in our practices when exploring the world.

The Role of the Pineal Gland

The pineal gland is an endocrine gland that is responsible in producing melatonin. Melatonin is that hormone which is responsible for the wake-sleep patterns and seasonal functions. Also called the third eye, the pineal gland is located close to the center of the brain in between hemispheres. It is found in a channel that joins the two thalamic bodies.

The physiological functions of the pineal gland are still unknown but different mystical studies have looked deeper into this area of the brain. It is believed to be the bridge that connects the physical and spiritual world. The pineal gland is said to provide the strongest ethereal energy to humans and is the source of all supernatural powers. Psychic talents are acquired as a result of the development of the pineal gland. It is also linked to higher vision that enables one to see beyond visible light.

The third eye manipulates the different biological rhythms in the body and works closely with the hypothalamus to direct feelings of thirst or hunger, sexual desire, and control of biological clock to determine aging. Once the third eye is opened, one can feel pressure on the brain's base.

The deep location of the pineal gland in the brain seems to tell us so much about its importance. This gland has its own lens that enables us to see beyond the physical world. It increases the connection to the soul and empowers us to go beyond the visible light. Whether it is a meditation or visualization method, these out-of-body experiences can help enhance the functions of the third eye.

Chapter 2: The Pineal Gland and the Third Eye

As well as having physical qualities relating it to a biological eye, the pineal gland has many spiritual qualities, which have earned it the well-known name of the "third eye." Religions and traditions around the world have used symbolism that can be directly or indirectly linked to the pineal gland. Just how much the ancients understood regarding the role and function of the pineal gland remains a mystery. However, there seems to be a fair amount of evidence suggesting that they had at least some idea of how it affected a person's mood, creativity, dream cycle, and even certain psychic abilities. As a result, the health of the third eye was directly related to the health and wellbeing of a person's soul. This belief continues to be relevant in many traditions today, making the pineal gland one of the most spiritually important features of the human body.

The Third Eye Chakra

Similar to the endocrine system, the ancient Hindus recognized a system of energy centered in a person known as chakras. The term chakra comes from the Sanskrit word for wheel, which is how the Hindus depicted these energy centers. Each chakra was responsible for a particular type of energy, affecting specific elements of a person's life in both physical and spiritual terms. In fact, there was little difference in the Hindu mind between physical and spiritual health, as the one directly affected the other.

The pineal gland is the sixth of the seven chakras, located along an axis that travels up the center of a person's body from their groin to the crown of their head. It is pictured just between the eyebrows, only slightly higher than a person's physical eyes. Known as the third eye chakra, this was where the energy for seeing into the spirit world was created and managed. A sick or imbalanced chakra would result in low energy levels, causing a lack of clear thinking, imagination, intuition and spiritual insight. Essentially, a defective third eye chakra kept a person rooted in physical reality and virtually blind to the spirit world. Therefore, it was of the utmost importance to keep this chakra clean, healthy and performing at maximum efficiency.

The Seat of the Soul

The spiritual nature of the pineal gland also found its way into western cultures in a very real and meaningful way. Seventeenth-century French philosopher René Descartes referred to the pineal gland as the seat of the soul. It was his belief that this was where the actual mind of a person resided, at the very center of the brain. It is possible that his reference was the result of the fact that numerous religions used the pinecone as an image of divinity and spirituality. The symbol of the pinecone can be seen in such cultures as Greek, Roman, Egyptian, Aztec, Hindu, and others reaching back into the far recesses of human history. That the pineal gland is both shaped and named after the pinecone is something that would not have escaped the attention of a great thinker like Descartes.

Numerous others have contemplated the possible significance of pinecone symbolism in just about every major religion known to man. That a part of the brain was shaped this way was of enormous importance. After all, one of the most signifivant questions asked throughout the ages was the relationship between the soul and the body. Where does the one exist within the other? While this question has yet to be definitively answered, the pineal gland offered perhaps the best solution considered so far. After all, the soul was usually associated with such things as a person's mood, imagination, dreams, and creative spark. Therefore, since the pineal gland was responsible for these things it stood to reason that this was the virtual seat of a person's soul.

The Gateway between Body and Soul

Terms such as "seat of the soul" and "third eye" can make the pineal gland a spiritual noun of sorts. Such a notion, while technically true, would significantly undermine the importance of the pineal gland. The fact is that the pineal gland is the point where the two worlds of matter and spirit collide. In this light, the pineal gland can be seen as the gateway between body and soul. Thus, this is where the symbiotic relationship between body and soul can best be experienced.

This relationship can be witnessed in the fact that physical health and wellbeing can impact the soul and vise versa. On the one hand, when you engage in certain harmful behaviors and activities, which will be discussed later in the book, the performance of your pineal gland can suffer. As a result, your mental and spiritual health and wellbeing will also suffer. Alternatively, when your spiritual activities are negative or lacking your physical wellbeing will suffer as a result. This isn't just a matter of spiritual belief or mystical conjecture; it is the conclusion of medical professionals and psychologists from all around the world.

Interestingly enough, just as harmful activity on one end of the spectrum affects the other end negatively, so too, positive behaviors can have an equally positive impact. Thus, if you begin to eat healthy foods and do other physical activities to improve the health of your pineal gland your mental and spiritual well-being will improve. Alternatively, if you begin to engage in mental and spiritual activities that are positive and nurturing you will improve your physical condition. This relationship between spiritual and physical reality may be the single greatest wonder of the pineal gland and the functions it serves.

Chapter 3: What Is the Third Eye Chakra?

The Third Eye chakra, also often referred to as the sixth chakra Ajna, is the chakra that focuses on one's ability to see the deeper meaning in life's moments. This chakra can be summarized of the chakra of understanding, the chakra that works towards the ability to see beyond the material or "real" world.

Biologically, the Third Eye is referred to as the pineal gland within one's brain. The pineal gland produces and regulates melatonin, which is the hormone responsible for our sleep/wake cycles and how we handle external stressors. Philosopher Descartes has described the pineal gland as "the principal seat of the soul". The pituitary gland is also important to Third Eye awakening and the sixth chakra in general, as it is responsible for multiple other hormone glands in the body. The pituitary gland, in biology, is often referred to as the "master gland".

When the Third Eye chakra is fully balanced or has been activated, both of your brain's hemispheres are able to function with complete synchrony. The Third Eye is sometimes referred to as our body's spiritual center, and works diligently to break down thoughts that have been brought on by illusion, strength, and fear; in order to open the mind to promote spiritual healing. The Third Eye differentiates what we believe to be true with what we know to be factual (or what really is true). This chakra houses your psychological skills as well as mental abilities and determines how we evaluate certain situations, attitudes, and beliefs.

The Third Eye is about not only the idea of seeing but more deeply than that the idea of truly understanding what is. This chakra is the source of our sense of ethics, morality, and justice (the Third Eye has also been said to be the part of us that receives messages from spiritual guides). Psychological functions associated with the Third Eye (or the pineal gland) are those of intuition and imagination.

There are numerous benefits to awakening your sixth chakra, or Third Eye, and below we have listed four ways for you to open your Third Eye followed by five signs that your Third Eye is opening.

How to Open the Third Eye:

1) **Touch-** Using your index finger, gently touch the area of your forehead located directly between your eyebrows. Rub this small spot in slow circles as you breathe

deeply (inhaling and exhaling slowly), and imagine the chakra opening.

2) **Essential Oils:** Using essential oils is a great way to relax while working to awaken your Third Eye. Essential oils can be used to promote general wellness while you are sleeping or meditating to balance your chakras. Using an oil diffuser, diffuse several drops of sandalwood, chamomile, or myrrh in order to promote the awakening of your Third Eye.

(3) **Breathe:** This technique can be used continuously throughout the day to promote the opening of your Third Eye. Many people practice the bad habit of shallow breathing without even realizing. In order to effectively awaken your sixth

chakra, it is important that you focus on and regularly practice deep breathing. When inhaling, be sure that you are breathing deep enough that your abdomen expands with each breathe.

(4) **Clairvoyance Meditation:** To practice this technique, find a comfortable spot to sit and relax your body completely. Once relaxed in a sitting position, practice the deep breathing mentioned above for several minutes. Next, visualize the number 1 in the center of your head between your eyebrows (while still utilizing the deep breathing exercises). Once you have clearly visualized the number 1, move up to the number 2, and repeat this exercise up to the number 10. This meditation exercise will help practice not only relaxation and breathing techniques but also can help to practice clearly visualizing different shapes and symbols.

Five Signs the Third Eye is Open:

Once you begin regularly exercising your mental strength to attempt to open the Third Eye, you may notice certain changes in the way you see or perceive things. Below are five signs or symptoms that you may notice and often act as a sign that you are becoming successful in awakening your Third Eye:

(1) You may feel a gentle pressure or spread of warmth between your eyebrows when encouraging your Third Eye to open.

(2) You may notice an increased feeling of intuition, or a stronger "feeling" about what is right to do when you are faced with making a decision.

(3) As you encourage your Third Eye to awaken, you may begin to notice a slight sensitivity to bright light.

(4) You may feel a continuous feeling of change within yourself (body and mind).

(5) As your Third Eye begins to open or awaken, you may experience mild headaches, though these typically occur

less and less frequently as you continue exercising opening your Third Eye.

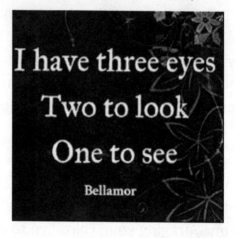

I have three eyes
Two to look
One to see

Bellamor

Chapter 4: How to awaken your third eye

Step by step instructions to Open Your Third Eye

In Hinduism, the third eye symbolizes a higher condition of cognizance through which you can see the world. Utilizing conventional reflection strategies, you can open up this chakra and addition a more profound, increasingly edified comprehension of the universe around you.

Find your third eye chakra. Chakras are the vitality focuses in your body. Basically, that are wheels of vitality that adjust along your spine. There are seven chakras, and each compares to an alternate piece of your physical, mental, and otherworldly prosperity. Your third eye chakra is the 6th chakra.The third eye chakra is situated at the bleeding edge of your mind, between your two eyes. It is directly over the extension of your nose. At the point when you ponder, attempt to concentrate your psyche on this chakra. It is liable for helping you to see the world all the more obviously.

Pick the correct environment. Contemplation is one of the best devices for helping you to open your third eye. By carrying more attention to your musings, you will have the option to all the more likely access the psychological clearness that is related with the third eye. The center objective of reflection is to expedite the psyche to rest one idea or item. It is critical to pick surroundings where you feel good when you are starting to meditate.A few people feel increasingly serene and liberal when they are out in nature. In the event that this seems like you, you should seriously mull over reflecting outside. Discover a space that is the correct temperature and where you can sit without being upset by others.

Indoor contemplation is additionally splendidly fine. Numerous individuals have an assigned reflection space in their home. This for the most part incorporates a pad that makes it progressively agreeable to sit on the floor, and maybe a few candles and calming music.

Recollect that contemplation is an individual procedure. You ought to pick the surroundings that are directly for you.

Set up your stance. The mind-body association is significant in contemplation. The more agreeable you are physically, the simpler it will be to concentrate on you contemplation item or thought. The best reflection pose is by and large idea to be some variety of sitting leg over leg on the ground. On the off chance that you are accustomed to sitting in a seat, take some time every day to become accustomed to sitting on the floor. In time, it will feel progressively common it will be simpler to concentrate on your contemplation. A great many people decide to use in any event one pad to make sitting on the ground progressively agreeable. Don't hesitate to utilize a few strong pads on the off chance that you discover this works better for you. On the off chance that you basically can't be open to sitting, don't stress. You can attempt what is known as strolling contemplation. For certain individuals, the cadenced hints of their footfalls can be exceptionally calming. Walk gradually, and have a make way with the goal that you don't need to ponder where you are going.

Pick a reflection object. A contemplation article can be an idea or a physical item. The purpose of picking one is to make it simpler for your mind to center. This will prevent your contemplations from meandering and will make your reflection more effective.Candles are a mainstream contemplation object. The gleaming fire is anything but difficult to take a gander at and are soothing to numerous individuals. Your contemplation object doesn't need to be close by physically. Don't hesitate to picture the sea or a lovely tree that you once observed. Simply ensure you can plainly observe the article in your inner consciousness.

Pick a mantra. A mantra is a word or expression that you will continue during your reflection practice. You may state the mantra inside or for all to hear - that is an individual inclination. Your mantra ought to be something that is close to home and significant to you.Your mantra ought to be something that you need to coordinate into your psyche, or your mindfulness. For instance, you may decide to rehash, "I pick satisfaction". This will help fortify the possibility that you are going to concentrate on feeling delight for the duration of the day.

Another mantra thought is to pick only single word. For instance, you could rehash "harmony".

Make it an everyday practice. Contemplation is a training. That implies that the first run through to plunk down to reflect, it probably won't be a major achievement. Your brain may meander, or you may even nod off. Figuring out how to effectively ruminate is a procedure and it takes time.

Make contemplation a piece of your consistently life. Start with exceptionally little additions, possibly five minutes or even only two. Before long you will feel increasingly good with the procedure and have the option to commit more opportunity to contemplation every day.

Realize being careful. Being careful implies that you are all the more effectively mindful of what is happening around you. You are intentionally focusing on your feelings and physical sensations. Being increasingly careful will assist you with getting on top of yourself and the world around you.As you are getting increasingly attentive, abstain from being judgemental. Simply watch and recognize without shaping a supposition about in the case of something is "correct" or "wrong".

For instance, on the off chance that you are getting a handle on pushed, don't pass judgment on yourself for feeling that way. Basically watch and recognize your feelings.

Head outside. Investing some energy outside can be extremely useful in getting progressively careful. Being progressively careful can assist you with opening your third eye since you will be increasingly mindful of it. Along these lines, it's a smart thought to attempt to go for a short stroll every day, with an end goal to invest more energy in nature.In the present culture, we are "connected" for quite a bit of our day. This implies we are quite often taking a gander at some kind of electronic or specialized gadget. Going outside reminds us to effectively take a break from the entirety of the improvements.

Be innovative. Being careful can enable you to get more in contact with your innovative side. Research proposes that careful reflection is an incredible remedy for author's squares and for hinders that craftsmen and other innovative sorts understanding. Being increasingly careful can enable you to open up your inventive pathways.Take a stab at trying different things with your innovative side. Take up painting, outlining, or learning another instrument. Letting your inventiveness stream will assist you with feeling more on top of yourself, and help you to open your third eye.

Concentrate on the little things. Everyday life can feel exceptionally chaotic and overpowering. Being increasingly careful can assist you with feeling quieter and better ready to use your third eye. Focus on every part of your environment and your routine.For instance, when you are scrubbing down, deliberately watch the physical sensations. Observe how the warm water feels on your shoulders. Welcome the reviving aroma of your cleanser.

Feel progressively tranquil. When you figure out how to open your third eye, you will have the option to encounter the advantages that accompany it. Numerous individuals report feeling more settled subsequent to opening their third eye. Some portion of this is expected to accomplishing a more noteworthy feeling of self-sympathy. Being increasingly mindful of yourself by and large makes you practice progressively self-kindness.

Being kinder to yourself offers numerous advantages. You will feel progressively fearless and less restless. Be progressively learned. One reason numerous individuals need to open their third eye is on the grounds that it is thought to make you increasingly proficient. Since it expands your impression of your general surroundings, it bodes well that you will have the option to become familiar with your general surroundings. Individuals who have opened their third eye report that they sense that they have more wisdom.

You will likewise turn out to be progressively learned about yourself. Contemplation and care are extraordinary approaches to connect with yourself. At the point when you better comprehend your feelings, you will feel increasingly equipped for managing them.

Improve your physical wellbeing. Opening your third eye is probably going to lessen your feelings of anxiety. You will feel increasingly serene and mindful. There are numerous physical advantages from diminished degrees of stress. Individuals with less pressure are less inclined to have hypertension and indications of depression.

Encountering less pressure can likewise mean a decrease in things, for example, cerebral pains and upset stomachs. It can even assist you with having more youthful looking skin.

Third Eye Chakra Healing For Beginners: How To Open Your Third Eye

At the point when you initially catch wind of chakras, the idea can sound confounding. You may ponder precisely where all these chakras, including the third eye chakra, should be. In addition, how might we impact them? Do you need to turn into a contemplation ace to utilize them for recuperating? Therefore, you may feel enticed to simply proceed onward to another kind of mending work.

Nonetheless, opening chakras doesn't have to include long stretches of examining or practice. This manual for chakras for apprentices will concentrate on third eye arousing, specifically, investigating how you can recognize and evacuate squares to your third eye chakra. As it were, figuring out how to do third eye chakra practices sets you up for progressively complex chakra mending later on. This is on the grounds that the third eye chakra is tied in with sharpening your instinct and adjusting to the more extensive universe.

What Is a Chakra? Third Eye Chakra Meaning and Location

7-chakrasBefore we investigate how to know whether your third eye is open, it's critical to comprehend that the third eye chakra is one of seven individual chakras.

Running from the root chakra at the base of the spine to the crown chakra at the highest point of the head, every one of the seven chakras are amazing vitality focuses.

The point is to utilize chakra activities to keep all these vitality focuses open and adjusted. In the event that you can accomplish this, you'll be better ready to satisfy your maximum capacity and carry on with an upbeat life. Conversely, the more chakras are blocked or skewed, the more you'll detect something isn't right.

Third Eye Chakra Information Summary

Physical Location: In the focal point of your forehead.

Shading: Indigo.

Component: Extra-Sensory Perception.

Related Animal: Black Antelope.

Intense subject matters and Behaviors of Blocked Third Eye Chakra: When your Third Eye Chakra is blocked, you may battle to have confidence in your more extensive reason. In this way, you may feel there's no good reason for what you're doing, or feel it is inconsequential. You may likewise be struck by your powerlessness to decide. A few people depict this as a sentiment of mental loss of motion. On the off chance that you have a blocked Third Eye Chakra, you may experience difficulty resting, feel awkward, and battle to adapt new things.

Adjusting Chakras: What Is The Third Eye Chakra Responsible For?

The third eye chakra (or the Ajna chakra) sits between your foreheads, and it is associated with your otherworldliness, extensively translated.

Given the Ajna's significance, the third eye's parity influences (and is influenced by) the entirety of the accompanying things:

Your capacity to frame precise hunches.

Your feeling of the master plan throughout everyday life.

Regardless of whether you meet objectives identified with your most profound reason.

Adjusting feeling and reason.

Regardless of whether you feel you're dormant or pushing ahead.

In this way, when your third eye is open, you will utilize the two emotions and rationale to settle on critical choices throughout everyday life. You will trust in your very own instincts, and you will be happy with realizing that you're experiencing your motivation. At the point when you practice third eye chakra mending, you can see a significant distinction in your amends with your general surroundings, and on your capacity to be careful.

At the point when you're managing a third eye chakra blockage, you can begin to get negative third eye chakra indications. This can create when something makes you question your instinct's exactness, or when something gives you motivation to address what you thought was your motivation.

(For a large number of years, light specialists and vitality healers have utilized explicit stones to quiet and center the psyche, decrease pressure, and cultivate wellbeing and essentialness. Discover more and get your free vitality arm ornament, simply click here now to discover more...)

Manifestations of a Blocked Third Eye Chakra

Nobody experiences existence without pondering how to unblock chakras once in a while. Along these lines, don't stress if third eye chakra recuperating must be performed over and again.

The most significant thing is simply to have the option to recognize signs and manifestations of third eye chakra issues with the goal that you follow up on them as quickly as time permits. Here are the absolute generally normal:

Absence of confidence in your motivation

Feeling futile

Hesitation

Finding your work or life irrelevant

Suspicion

Third eye blockages can likewise trigger a scope of inconvenient physical side effects. The most much of the time revealed include:

Cerebral pains (counting headaches)

Eye uneasiness

Back and leg torment

Sinus torment

Everybody has various triggers that sparkle the requirement for third eye recuperating. Be that as it may, it's valuable to know about the absolute most regular reasons for blockages in the third eye.

For instance, when somebody puts down your employment or enthusiasm, this can push the third eye chakra lopsided.

Likewise, experiencing a transitional beneficial encounter like sickness, passing, work misfortune or separation can make a blockage. Indeed, even simply moving into another period (for example around a huge birthday) affects your third eye chakra, given that it is so delicate to your view of your life's worth.

Third Eye Chakra Healing: How To Open And Unblock Your Third Eye Chakra

AjnaThird eye mending isn't as cloudy or mind boggling as it may sound. While the third enlightening experience can be significant, the kinds of systems that open the third eye chakra are shockingly straightforward.

We'll investigate four of the most helpful and clear approaches to gain by your new comprehension of the third eye's significance.

The entirety of the accompanying activities center around how to adjust your chakras, with an accentuation on the third eye chakra specifically.

In the event that you need some additional inspiration for utilizing and more than once rehearsing these strategies, simply recall that an unblocked third eye chakra can be the way in to a more joyful life. At the point when you have a finely tuned feeling of instinct, you normally float towards the open doors that are directly for you. What's more, monitoring third enlightening side effects is a simple method to tell whether you are living as per your actual reason.

1. Utilize Third Eye Chakra Stones And Jewelry For Healing

There is a chakra hues test that binds different various shades to various chakras. For the third eye chakra, the key shading is purple. This gives you helpful data to discovering third eye chakra stones to work with.

The idea is that you can discover adornments including purple stones and wear it whenever you have to unblock the third eye chakra. You can likewise buy bigger third eye gems that will sit in your pocket or in the palm of your hand, enabling you to crush them and spotlight on them when you have to keep your third eye chakra open.

Probably the best third eye stones incorporate the accompanying:

Purple fluorite: This semi-valuable jewel should elevate honed instinct and to clear up obfuscated contemplations. It's a perfect third eye chakra precious stone when you're attempting to settle on a troublesome decision and need to dispose of insignificant interruptions.

Amethyst: An acclaimed and lovely valuable stone, amethyst is customarily associated with third eye migraine help just as all types of mending. A few people additionally use it to speak to shrewdness.

Dark Obsidian: Another well known individual from the third eye precious stones gathering, dark obsidian advances balance among feeling and reason.

2. Third Eye Chakra Meditation And Yoga Techniques

Reflection may be one of the main things that rung a bell when you think about the inquiry "What is a chakra?". Notwithstanding, third eye reflection is only one of numerous approaches to take a shot at opening this chakra. Also, there are a lot of chakra contemplation methods for amateurs don't as well, stress on the off chance that you've never attempted care or reflection. Here's one to begin with:

Sit serenely and close your eyes. Breathe in and breathe out multiple times, gradually and profoundly. Concentrate on the area of the third eye chakra, envision a violet circle of vitality in your temple. Keep in mind, purple is the third eye chakra's shading. As you keep on breathing gradually and profoundly, picture the purple wad of vitality getting greater and hotter. As it does, envision it cleansing antagonism from your body.

Consider yourself of engrossing the third eye chakra's vitality—enable yourself to feel it everywhere.

Open your eyes when you feel prepared.

As you may have speculated, yoga can likewise be useful when figuring out how to adjust your chakras. Third eye yoga presents incorporate the youngster present and the bird present. You can discover pictures and recordings that will manage you through these clear positions. You may see third eye chakra opening side effects before long!

3. Chakra Foods List And Diet Suggestions

As is natural, fundamental chakra nourishments (for example ones that help all chakras) are for the most part sound staples. For instance, all organic products, vegetables, sound fats and wholegrain nourishments will in general advance transparency all through the chakra framework.

Be that as it may, there are additionally explicit third eye chakra nourishments, and adding them to your every day diet can anticipate or battle blockages. Remember the accompanying:

Dull chocolate: If you like dim chocolate, don't hesitate to have as much as you need when you're attempting to open the third eye! It is said to help improve mental clearness and lift fixation. It is an extraordinary wellspring of magnesium, which destresses you. As a little something extra, it advances the arrival of serotonin, placing you in a progressively positive disposition.

Anything purple: Given that purple is the third eye's shading, every single purple nourishment advance its equalization. The absolute best models incorporate eggplant, purple cabbage, red grapes, blueberries, and blackberries.

Omega-3: Foods that are wealthy in omega-3 can improve subjective capacity and along these lines help to keep your third eye chakra open. Great decisions incorporate pecans, salmon, chia seeds and sardines.

(Consideration: Energy mending searchers, get this mind blowing 'Reiki Energy Healing Bracelet' for nothing! Snap here now to get yours.)

4. Third Eye Chakra Affirmations To Use

Confirmations are phrases that target negative, restricting convictions and supplant them with increasingly positive convictions. They can be utilized to assist you including weight reduction to discovering love, so it makes sense that they can likewise be utilized to adjust chakras.

three-tips-for-making amazing attestations

When structuring third eye attestations, specifically, you need to concentrate on otherworldliness, your gut impulses, and your fundamental feeling of direction. Here are a few models you can attempt.

Don't hesitate to change them until they feel right:

"I pursue the lead of my inward instructor."

"I realize how to settle on the correct choices, and I do as such effortlessly."

"I hear my instincts and I realize they will lead me to my motivation."

"I am on my actual way."

"I live each day as per my life's motivation."

"I confide in the direction that my third eye gives me."

"I have boundless conceivable outcomes accessible to me."

"I am an instinctive individual, and I realize what is directly for me."

"It is sheltered and great to pursue the direction of my third eye."

"My third eye is open and prepared to see my motivation."

Chapter 5: Opening the Third Eye

You've definitely heard about it, but do you really know what third eye means? Of course it is not physically having a third eye magically appearing just above the area between your "real" eyes.

What is the "third eye"?
The third eye is also referred to as the inner eye. It is actually a concept that refers to the invisible speculative "eye" often depicted as being located on the forehead. It provides perception beyond what you see with the naked eye.

Other religions and spiritual traditions have different names for the third eye. In Hinduism, it is called the **chakra, ajna,** or **brow.** In Theosophy, it is associated with the pineal gland. The third eye is like a gate that is perceived to lead you to the inner realms of higher consciousness.

New Age followers, on the other hand, refer to the third eye as a symbol for a state of enlightenment.

A lot of people associate the third eye with clairvoyance, visions, precognition, and the ability to see auras and chakras. The people who use their third eyes are referred to as **seers.**

Accessing Your Third eye

The third eye is associated with one's ability to see what is not seen. Most often, people believe that the third eye is one's intuition. How many times have you changed plans or decisions in the past because of a hunch? For instance, you were supposed to go out the night before but decided against it because you felt uneasy and your gut told you to just stay home. Then you heard in the news that an untoward accident happened in the same bar that you were supposed to have gone to that night. That is intuition!

There are some people who have "open" third eyes while there are others who aren't. But everyone has it and can tap onto it anytime they want to. It is a natural part of every human being.

Many people with "open" third eyes use theirs for different purposes. Seers use them to be able to understand certain events and how they might be connected to a certain person. Seers usually use their third eyes to answer questions that have long been unanswered.

For some, they use theirs to "feel" energies and thereby being able to manipulate them.

Chapter 6: What Is the Third Eye?

The 'third eye' is a spiritual center in your body that is responsible for inner wisdom and guidance. Our third eye gives us the ability to see the things that could be and is responsible for so-called 'gut feelings' and 'hunches.' Everybody has a third eye, but people will experience it differently depending on their personal awareness, belief, and faith in it.

First, let's discuss the origins of the third eye. The spiritual third eye refers to the chakra system originally developed as part of Kundalini yoga but has been the focus of many Indian and Asian practices for centuries. The premise is simple. Energy flows all around us. The universe is made of energy, we are made of energy. There are seven main chakras, or 'energy centers,' within the body, and they all align with the center of the body. [1]

Each chakra is said to be responsible for different aspects of physical health, emotional well-being, and our harmony with the world. For example, the root chakra is located at the base of the spine, on our tailbone. This chakra is said to be responsible for grounding, and a misaligned chakra could mean that you are having trouble finding meaning in your life, have difficulty holding down a job or finding a suitable place to live, and it even has physical ramifications.

Aligning your chakras and making sure that energy is properly flowing through each is the key to good health and a prosperous happy life, according to Kundalini practices. For the sake of this book, we will focus mostly on the third eye chakra. This energy center is located between the eyes, just a little bit above. If you could see it physically, it would look as if you had a third eye.

This reference isn't just physical, however. The spiritual third eye corresponds to your ability to see more clearly. Your two physical eyes can see objects in front of you, but your third eye senses energy, auras, and has the ultimate spiritual wisdom. Using your third eye as a spiritual compass, there is nothing you can't conquer.

The spiritual aspects of the third eye may be hard to grasp, especially if you have not yet discovered its potential in you. However, the third eye isn't just spiritual, it actually corresponds to a physical entity within your brain. The pineal gland is a small walnut-sized gland located in the center of your brain. If you were to look someone square in the forehead, the pineal gland is located just behind the spiritual third eye.

This small gland has always been a medical mystery. It is hard to get to, and therefore, hard to test. We have only scratched the surface of what purposes this small gland could be for. What we do know is that this gland is responsible for producing melatonin, a hormone that regulates sleeping, waking patterns, and the circadian rhythm.

Without a properly-functioning pineal gland, the body would not know when to wake and sleep naturally, throwing the natural course of time in an individual off balance. We all know that having enough sleep ensures you have good health while a lack of sleep can have many negative effects.

We have all been in a spot where a bad night of sleep ruins our following day. We walk around listlessly, unable to gather enough energy or motivation to deal with everyday tasks, and all we think about is sleep. Then, once bedtime rolls around again, we are wide awake, and the bad cycle continues.

This irregular pattern of sleep can affect us down to the cellular level. Lack of sleep creates stress on the body which triggers the release of stress hormones like cortisol and adrenaline. These hormones raise blood pressure, stress the heart, call for more storage of fat, and general low-level inflammation affects cells all over the body.

Stress has long been understood as a cause of premature aging. As the stress affects your body's cells, it makes them susceptible to the point that it results in a shorter cell life, greater turnover, and a quicker route to eventual cell death.

On a more spiritual level, the third eye is thought to be a center of wisdom. It is this chakra's connection with the energy of the universe that makes it all-knowing and all-seeing. If we are able to harness this energy and actually listen when this chakra is trying to guide us, it helps us make good decisions that bring us closer to spiritual enlightenment.

Depending on whom you will ask, this chakra can also be thought of as our 'inner-self,' or our soul. This is the part of us who deep down knows all of our deepest thoughts and desires. It is what keeps us going toward our goals and dreams, even if we don't know it's happening.

We have all had those feelings of overwhelming happiness, and also dread. Some situations lend to these feelings automatically, but if you have ever felt unexplainably uneasy about something, this is a signal that your third eye chakra is trying to sway you from whatever situation you are in.

These signals should not be ignored. Our inner self can see ahead, and while it may seem like you are on the right track now, the infinite wisdom of the universe, conveyed through your third eye, can tell the difference between temporary happiness and eternal freedom.

This seems like such a powerful force, so why are so many people off track and out of balance with their third eye chakra? Our modern society is very focused on the facts of tangible science as a way to solve our problems. We use medicine and medical procedures to cure ailments while mental and spiritual health are largely misunderstood. We are not taught as children to connect with our inner-self, to go with our gut feelings, we are meant to follow the rules of society, whether they conflict with our inner wisdom or not.

The third eye is, technically speaking, almost extinct. However, there is an overwhelming need for infinite wisdom in the world, and each individual should learn to tap into theirs.

When it comes to the physical pineal gland, it is necessary to care for it just as you would your heart. We intend to eat healthily and exercise to take care of our [2]hearts, but our pineal glands are subject to disrepair as well. There is evidence that a pineal gland can become calcified, a physical buildup of mineral and toxic film that encapsulates the gland.

When this happens, a disruption in melatonin production occurs, and it hinders the gland from working correctly.

On a spiritual level, consider that you are putting an eye patch over your third eye. If it can't see, it cannot help guide you. If you have ever felt aimless in life or felt unsure where to go next while other people around you seem to be driven and successful, it could be that your third eye cannot see and that you are making your way through life without its infinite guidance.

Chapter 7: Process of Unlocking the Third Eye

Electro-magnetic field pollution can be among the most influential Pollution and can be emitted by cell phones, Wi-Fi, microwaves, transmission masts, power grids etc. and they interfere with our regular connection to nature's frequencies keeping us in an artificial Electro Magnetic field frequency.

The most effective brain wave that is transmitted emulates natural frequencies of the earth and interchangeably too without the pollution from the Electro Magnetic field pollution.

The brain wave listening when carried out in an environment void of the Electro Magnetic field pollution would mean awakening the third eye and the crown chakras which are the Spiritual links from the physical world. By unlocking the pineal gland, after a few weeks of brain wave transmission meditation, getting into a higher level of meditative state would not require brain wave in transmit anymore.

The true nature of our reality is then realized by focusing deep and reaching deep brain waves zones one can tap into the core of the universe's infinite knowledge.

This would in turn make our reality fit in together and make all the connections be observed. The potential to overcome hazardous effects that keeps many individuals from achieving this level of awakening include lack of proper exercising, poor diet, and diseases introduction into the body. Opening the third eye enhances the confidence of an individual and the method of achieving higher consciousness all of which meditation is an effective means of reaching.

Process of achieving this third eye opening and early experiences include feeling a light sensation within the first twenty minutes of the brain wave meditation which is felt at the location of the third eye Chakra.

This is the first step in achieving awakening the third eye. The boosting of the pineal glands makes it function during the first meditation. The stimulation of the pineal glands is similar to an exercise practice that takes place in the brain. With each meditation sessions, the toxins become removed and the individual becomes stronger and reaches a deeper level of extra sensory perceptions.

The slight pressure in the third eye Chakra region reduces after a few weeks, then the next effect is seeing vivid dark energy which looks like moving shadows or as others would put it, spirits but it has actually not been confirmed as to what it is exactly.

Immersion in warm water, in a semi dark room listening to the brain wave frequency enhances the meditation, some people claim to hear voices while others see the dark energy moving. These effects are subjective to individual differences

AWAKENING THE ETHERIC CHAKRAS

When the chakras are activated starting with the sacral Chakra, man is reminded partially about his Astral traveling although this is only a slight stimulation of the Chakra and man only even vaguely remembers.

This feeling is like flying through the atmosphere and comes in bits of different forms and the man might not fully comprehend it at the early stages.

As the solar plexus Chakra becomes awakened, the individual starts to become aware physically of the effects of the Astral World in his physical sense.

In the awakening of the heart Chakra, the individual becomes conscious of other people's happiness or sadness intuitively and often times, he feels the emotions they feel and can recreate the replica feeling in himself.

The awakening of the throat Chakra, wakes up the individual's abilities to hear voices vividly, and this voices make advices to him at times, he could possibly hear songs or some sounds he cannot describe and this ability is called being Clairaudient and is Developed in the etheric planes.

In the activation of the third eye Chakra, the man begins to see images clearly and have visions, some unexplainable, some of events occurring. During its early stages, the images are on form of flashes but eventually become full realized images which is referred to as clairvoyance.

This Chakra also makes the physical eye more advanced, improving the magnification and sight overall and helps one to examine images in contraction and expansion. Prior to this full realization of the clairvoyance, the individual is likely to see frequent flashes of images of the celestial, this is due to signals being received from vibrations from one Chakra or another.

This imagery would consistently show up until eventually the clairvoyance is fully achieved and the individual can clearly see images at will during meditation stages.

Depending on how deep a brain wave meditation is, an individual would see clear images and hear vivid voices from the celestial world when the exchange of energy forces is in play and the chakras active.

AWAKENING THE CHAKRAS BEFORE ITS TIME

For the majority, the teachings about the chakras and energy flow and all are just nay saying and heresy and thus most don't believe in it and would probably never get to awaken these chakras.

Well, in a sense, it is better for these individuals to not awaken them and remain unaware of them as they remain laying in an inactive state as pertaining to their etheric use and not in connection to their physicality functionalities, as every human does require the chakras for normal existentiality as the energy flowing within them are required for normal activity and vitality as well.

Their spiritual qualities though, might never be utilized by the unaware and skeptics which is not bad as many, if not most of the people would end up living their lives without even having an idea what the chakras mean and they would still be fine Physically. It is the yearning for some spiritual connection that would be lost in people and the urge would go and remain unfulfilled in most of these individuals.

These regular people that never get to awaken these chakras and have them remain dormant are better off than those that awaken it prematurely before it's time. Awakening the chakras which are spiritual channels simply means attempting or even activating the Chakras before first developing a certain moral conduct which is more or less a necessity in unlocking the chakras in the first place.

Some of the effects can affect the individuals who awaken these spiritual channels prematurely in harmful ways. It may lead to effects which may be manifested physically and thus leaving them in pain, and this is even the lenient effect as some other adverse effects could be more than just physical injuries and may cause permanent havoc to the chakras in etheric plane themselves. Another effect common with awakening it before its time is that it streams the energy flow downward instead of the normal upward flow and this would over supply some points, hence causing the traits associated with these points to be over exhibited in the negative sense because it is an unbalance in the Chakra and could eventually lead to wreaking havoc in the body system of the individual if he doesn't take into full caution.

Possibilities of the individual attaining supernatural qualities are true, but these abilities go out of his control and he eventually regrets unlocking the chakras without following suit of how to best go about it. Unlocking the chakras untimely also leads to the Christ spark over activating the entire body system and this results in the individual being overpowered with the traits which reaches first the traits attributed to negativity before the traits attributed to positivity. These traits would be greatly interwoven as one would come with the other, i.e., the positive with the negative such as incisiveness and brilliance associated with pride and cunning.

AWAKENING OF THE CHRIST SPARK

The inner layers of this fire gets subconsciously lit up in some case and this may not even require a planning, but in such instances, the glow is dull, it may start some motion by itself, but this is rare. When this happens, serious pain may be involved, due to the passages not being ready for it, it is normally expected to clear the passage by using up a considerable amount of etheric abilities and this is not usually achieved without a deal of pain or suffering.

At this point, it comes down to a junction of no-pain-no-gain, and while the processes involve pain, the suffering process is not directly dangerous or harmful to our being, it's just an indicator of new paths being created, those that does not exist before. When the arousal is accidental and not planned, it attempts to move up the interior sessions of the spine, moving through the path already trekked by its manifestation, both the lowest and the highest.

This upward movement is totally necessary when possible but if it cannot be achieved, this is not serious need to worry, it will pop out to get expelled through the head into the immediate environment, this is not harmful but it will definitely cause a slight weakness in the body, this form of weakness has no permanent effect on the body and it will be gone within a few hours or a few days, all depending on the intensity of the whole process.

At the worst scenario possible, a loss of consciousness can occur but also, this is just temporary and will never lead to any permanent harm or death. All these dangers are not in any way connected to the upward rush in any sense, they are only connected to the possible of it turning downwards and inward. In occultism, the upward rush is known to make active the chakras and also establish strong connections between the astral and physical planes of the body, this connection is very paramount and cannot be underestimated. Once this spark gets to the center around the eyebrows and fully manifests, it comes with a power to hear, this hear is called voice of the master, with the master being the ego or higher self or advanced consciousness, it has also been noted as the voice of silence in several cases but regardless, this voice is an approval.

The pituitary body established all the communications links required within, known as astral vehicle, through with all forms of messages are sent and received through stable paths without complications.

At this stage, it's not only this Chakra that is required, other chakras have to be actively awakened, that's the only way the sub planes can be linked responsively, from one force center to another, once this is achieve, the communication and links are swift.

This development cannot be rushed; therefore, it should not be rushed, it must be given the chance to play out. Hereditary and adaption also counts at this stage, according to records and researches, it has been proven that some Indians achieve this at first instance but the fact that their body is more adaptable naturally, but in most cases, this stage has to be repeated over time to achieve the connection. Repetitions is key for procuring the serpent-fire of the Christ spark since the passages are new at every time and every event of incarnation.

These repetitions become extremely easy over time has the body is no longer strange to new vehicles being developed but it must be noted that the processes are totally different for different individuals and that no exact result has to be expect in any case, for instance, there have been cases where the higher self was seen and not heard, this is due to the variation in the process and personalities.

Also, connection to the higher self has many levels, for individuals, it may mean ego and for the ego, it may mean monad power and also for the monad, it may mean a spontaneous epiphany of the logos, this is to show the possibilities and layers, nothing is fixed in a direct other and experiences may differ from person to person.

Chapter 8: Energy Healing

Energy healing is more of a broad term since there are multiple techniques that can be used. It is not a new type of healing, but it goes back centuries to the ancient world.

Early practitioners of energy healing believed that people fell ill when the energy within their bodies became out of balance. In Japan and China, they have created comprehensive systems for medical treatment based on the body's energy levels. In addition to reiki, chakra healing and spiritual healing, the following are also types of energy healing:

Qigon[g]

This technique utilizes a combination of posture, breathing, sound, movement, self-massage and focused intent. The purpose is to improve both physical and mental health. When this technique is used, it opens the meridian flow of energy. When engaging in the movements, tendons, muscles, and ligaments are warmed, body fluid circulation is improved and connective tissues and internal organs are tonified.

Emotional Freedom Techniques
Also referred to as EFT, this healing technique can be used to improve the physical being and unresolved emotional issues. In terms of the physical, chronic pain is a common reason that someone might opt for this method. This technique is used to take advantage of the energy meridian points in the body. Using the fingertips, someone would tape the points. The healing power results from you

literally tapping into the energy that your body already possesses.

Biofield Energy
This technique is based on every person having a biofield. Various techniques are used to interact with it to alter a person's health in a positive way. The biofield is described as a type of energetic matrix of blueprint.

Therapeutic Touch
This technique is based on the belief that energy fields can be balanced or corrected via touch. However, when this is performed, the person is not actually physically touched. Instead, the practitioner places their hands close to body and uses their own energy to benefit the energy of the person they are working on. This technique has been studied and has been shown to be beneficial for promoting wound healing, reducing anxiety and alleviating pain. Other reasons this might be done include:

- Fibromyalgia
- Restless leg syndrome
- Bronchitis
- Lupus
- Chronic pain
- Sleep apnea
- Allergies
- Addictions
- Certain forms of dementia

Acupuncture

You have probably heard of acupuncture. It is a popular form of complementary medicine used for an array of ailments. In fact, many medical insurance companies even cover a set amount of sessions. It works based on the belief that when energy flow is disrupted in the body, disease can result. Acupuncture works to clear the disruptions so that energy is allowed to flow freely. One of the most prominent uses for this technique is pain and stress. Other possible uses that have shown promising results in research studies include:

- Nausea related to surgery or chemotherapy
- Addiction
- Headache
- Joint pain
- Fibromyalgia
- Osteoarthritis
- Carpal tunnel syndrome
- Stroke
- Menstrual cramps
- Myofascial pain
- Low back pain
- Asthma

Yoga

Yoga is a popular technique used by those looking to increase their mind-body connection. It can aid people in coping with stress. Other mental benefits can include:

- Improved calmness and mental clarity
- Relaxing the mind
- Sharpening concentration
- Increased body awareness
- Centering attention

Yoga can also help to promote better physical health. It is commonly used by those looking to lower their blood pressure, alleviate pain or reduce their insomnia. Other possible physical benefits can include:

- Increased flexibility
- Better energy, respiration and vitality
- Weight reduction
- Improved athletic performance
- Enhanced muscle tone and strength
- Balancing the metabolism
- Better circulatory and cardiovascular health
- Injury protection

Sufi Meditation

There are different types of this meditation practice and all of them are done to work toward achieving a mystical union with your preferred deity and to purify yourself.

Polarity Therapy

The purpose of this therapy is to balance and stimulate life energy flow in the body. Your energy has to continue to flow without becoming obstructed. When an obstruction occurs, this essentially throws the body out of balance. This therapy is focused on making the flow better so that the blocked energy is not able to cause issues with well-being.

Visualization

Visualization is often used during meditation. It allows you to essentially see yourself doing away with the bad and engaging with what is good. This is a popular technique and research shows that it can:

- Improve performance
- Reduce stress
- Increase the ability for you to reach you potential
- Enhances your overall joy
- Sparks your inspiration
- Enhances your ability to focus
- Boosts your confidence
- Reduces healing time from illness
- Alleviates nervousness
- Improves your creativity

Meditation Session #3: Water Meditation – 25 Minutes

Water has a naturally calming and tranquil effect. It is natural and relaxing, but also powerful. It is an element that is needed to sustain all forms of life. This meditation session taps into the unique qualities of water. You can choose to sit in a relaxing bath, out in the falling rain or in another body of water, such as a pool, lake or river. Let the movement of the water whisk away your negative emotions, thoughts and stresses. As you see the water moving, imagine it taking anything bad and moving it away. Feel the temperature of the water or the gentle touch of the rain drops as they fall. Put all of your focus on the water and it alleviating all of your emotional and mental stress.

CHAPTER 9: SIXTH-CHAKRA ABILITIES AND POSSIBILITIES

+ Uses instinct, zero.33 eye opens

+ Feels oneness with others

+ Hears others

+ Perceives totality of existence

+ Sees, hears, and senses very own internal

+ Alert and conscious

+ Hears messages from personal body

+ Taps into deep inner know-how

+ Uses insights about others for

+ Deep or significant communications

+ Detached from satisfaction related

+ Evolving recognition

Chapter 10: How to Balance This Chakra

· Meditation is a great way to develop and nurture your intuition.

· Aromatic essential oils such as Myrrh, Olibanum and even Patchouli are great for developing concentration.

· Try and use the color purple in your daily life. Say for example, wear a purple scarf or a purple top so as to increase the flow of energy.

· Opt for soothing classical music that will enable the flow of positive energy in your body.

· Amethyst, tanzanite, and tourmaline are popular stones that are associated with the Third Eye ,and you can easily wear them to balance the 6th chakra.

· Seek answers to questions that have been bugging you for a long time. Seek the answers from the Universe. You may to wait for a few seconds to several months before the answer is delivered to you. The answer can come from within as well, or there may be signs or incidents happening that will give answers to your questions.

· Keep a diary where you need to write down the dreams and visions that you are experiencing.

· Close your eyes, and let your body relax. Remain in this position for several minutes until you feel the external muscles relax around your eyes. Then slowly soften the muscles inside your eyes, allowing the sense of relaxation to penetrate deep inside your body. Try and notice the images appearing in your mind's eye.

· Try your hand at drawing. Or opt for another form of art that requires a high level of concentration and observation on your part.

· Try out star gazing.

· Repeat positive thoughts such as:

"My imagination is clear and vivid."

"My mind is agile and powerful."

"I have strong intuition and insight."

"I see and understand the bigger picture."

"My intellect is strong and useful."

"I envision good and positive images."

"I am open to the wisdom inside me."

"Greater spiritual awareness awaits me."

Chapter 11: Experiences After The Third Eye Opening

After the third eye opening you may get some unusual experiences.

Some of the experiences you may get are pleasant, some aren't. If you already opened the third eye, read about the experiences after the third eye opening. If your your third eye is not opened, read this section of the eBook.

How to know that you awakened your third eye

You can be assured that your third eye is awakened if you close your eyes and can see:

* White/blue/purple colours

* Intense white dots

* Black sky with numerous stars

* The shape of the eye/square/circle/some other shape filled with blue or purple colour

These are all signs that you've awakened your third eye.

If you feel the pressure or some activity in your third eye chakra, that means that your third eye is being awakened and soon you'll be able to see with it.

Chapter 12: Signs and Symptoms of Developing the Third Eye

You have often heard of the third eye activation and enlightenment. It is all about doing exercises mentally to connect with the third eye. This will in turn make the ability strong and active. Below are observable facts that you are likely to experience when you are developing your third eye:

-There is a change in eating habits such as obtaining a diet of greens and vegetables rather than meat.

-There is often that desire to meditate more often.

-If you close your eyes, you sometimes visualize clearly on things.

-During the night or when you wake up, you may see energy fields.

-You have a strong feeling of knowing people's past or present thoughts and intentions.

-You have a good feeling or always being optimistic.

-There is change in the way you sleep, an increase or decrease in sleep.

-Sometimes you see the future.

-You always want to do more research and read often.

-Experience feelings of learning content knowledge while in a dreaming state.

-You are well connected with nature especially the planet, plants and the earth.

-You become loving to yourself and to others.

-You get very sensitive when experiencing negative energy.

-You become very creative.

-You tend to make wise decisions.

Underactive Third Eye

The underactive third eye has the following signs:

-Confusion.

-Worry.

-Forgetfulness.

-Lack of discernment.

-Gland problems.

-Little or no psychic skills.

-Not being yourself.

-Focused on materialism.

Overactive Third Eye

If the eye is overactive, it can have psychic distress and be disoriented. An overactive third eye causes someone to feel lost in visions and having information that makes no sense. The third eye needs to be balanced for you to see things clearly make wise decisions, be focused and you can differentiate between dream and reality. Having an overactive third eye is the complete opposite of what it should be. The thoughts do come in often and cause mental exhaustion and you tend not to differentiate reality from a dream.

The signs that one has an overactive third eye include:

Physical signs

-Fatigue.

-Headache.

-Lack of focus.

-Confusion.

-Insomnia.

-Nausea.

-Sinusitis.

-Vision problems.

Emotional signs

-Depression.

-Fear.

-Delusion.

-Being judgmental.

-Hallucination.

-Anxiety.

-Panic attack.

For you to improve on the effect of overactive third eye, consider changing your lifestyle practices. For example: eating healthy foods, doing regular exercises, and practicing energy healing. All these are of essence in the balancing of the third eye.

Good luck!

Chapter 13: CRYSTALS THAT OPEN YOUR THIRD EYE CHAKRA

There are so many numerous tools that can be used to open and activate and balance your chakras system. This Third Eye chakra is your Sixth Sense, and it governs your intuition and your soul. It is associated with the color indigo, so there are specific stones that are associated with this chakra and if you use them, you could develop psychic abilities like clairvoyance, clear audience and intuition.

You should always cleanse your chakra Stones before using them, which includes smudging or burying them in a jar for a short time. When you're using crystals to balance your third eye crystal, it will take time before you begin to see the symptoms.

There are several healing stones that you can use to open your third eye chakra, and the Stones have different properties, so let us discuss some crystals that you can use to open your third eye chakra.

Clear Quartz Crystal

The first one is a clear quartz crystal. It is often called the master healer, and it works to enhance and clear away all your chakras. It will charge the energy of your order chakra and work tirelessly to enhance you while you're awaking you to your abilities. The stone will amplify and focus your energy and help you to be able to focus your energy on opening your abilities, the story has the power of your thoughts going out with the universe.

It's like taking a whisper and raising it up to the universe. The universe will hear you, and your intention will be answered. Quartz can enhance your spiritual growth and serves as a teacher to you on your part. It is a very powerful stone in terms of psychic protection. It will protect you from taking on the negativity of others, and it will protect you from negative energy and jealousy.

Lapiz Lazuli

The second stone is Lapis Lazuli. This stone is long-treasured, and it has been used for thousands of years for illumination and enlightenment. The stone will help you open your third eye with its specs of gold and dark blue colors, reminding you of the night sky where all is possible and Infinite.

The stone is the psychic stone of preference. It opens the mind from the conscience attachment. The powerful vibration of the stone will work as a protector and help to connect your mind to the soul part ways and provide mental transit along the lines that bind you together. It helps condition your energy to a higher vibration so that you can increase your spiritual progress. The stone also enhances your dream and helps you connect with your spirit guides. It is placed on the third eye to enhance psychic ability.

Labradorite

The third one is Labradorite. This is a very highly protective and spiritual stone. It will enhance and awaken your psychic ability while protecting your head high and shielding you from negative influences. Many psychics are impacted, which means that they feel the feelings of other people, and they take those feelings as their own. Labradorite is a supportive stone and it will help you to transform information to your head.

It can bring greater understanding and give you close observation of any struggles in your life. By placing the stone on the third eye during meditation, you'll be able to bring your intuition and intellect into balance. This stone can be used for past life work and answers to the cacique record. Continue working with this stone, and you'll be able to improve your skill of discernment. It can eliminate the illness of the brain and the eyes and it will help you regulate your metabolism.

Amethyst

The fourth one is Amethyst. This stone is used to enhance our spirituality, and it comes to your mind and allows your soul to awaken. This stone reminds you that you are one, and as you open your abilities, you are helping other people to do the same thing. It takes you to the next level of your spiritual development. This is the most common crystal stone used with the third eye chakra, and it is also used with the 10th chakra. It is a very powerful spiritual tool, which will help you bring balance and harmony to the Third Eye chakra and clear your mind and psychic opening.

This tune is also used for future prediction because of its ability to open the mind to the root causes behind addictive behaviors physically. It can help balance cell brains and nerve disorders. The Third Eye opens the gate from the brown to the crown of your body and beyond. For meditation, this stone has a suitable meditation component.

It can help you relax your mind and can reduce the stresses of the body, which can hinder your journey. If you sleep with this stone, you'll be able to remember your dreams easily. If you have a psychic child in your home, simply place this stone by the child's bed and it will protect him/her from negative dreams and help in understanding their natural abilities with patience and wisdom. The stone works best when it is near the body. So always try to carry it with you, but keep it next to your bedside.

Moonstone

The next stone is Moonstone. It is a highly mystical stone. If you need to develop psychic abilities that have been shut down due to fear, this is a good stone to use. This negative stone helps to absorb the power of the moon. It is important to always clean it's in the light of the full moon. In addition to enhancing your psychic ability, the stone also helps in protecting travelers, it observes tension in the home and regulates your body clock. It is also a great tool for women going through puberty, menopause, or pregnancy. It lessens mood swings and stops emotional imbalance, and it will help you to understand your psychic abilities.

Sodalite

The sixth one is Sodalite. Sodalite helps to calm the mind and conquers the thoughts that keep you distracted from the peace within. Once the mind is calm by the storm, the stone takes the mind to the highest mind so that the journey becomes easier for the mind. This stone is a spiritual stone that adheres to resonate strongly with the third eye chakra.

It has a way of calming the mind and any mental the degrees that are coupled with intuitive and spiritual perception. The stone also strengthens your self-esteem and self-trust as it eliminates fear and guilt, and help you to find a healthy emotional balance. The stone is the strong stone in the search for truth as it moves you towards the quality of being truthful to yourself and stand for what you believe in. Sodalite will help you to bring together both intuitive thought and logical thought so that you'll be able to find the right balance between your thoughts and your feelings.

Moldavite

The seventh stone is called Moldavite, modified as the Premier third Eye chakra stone. This stone works with all the chakras, and it is very popular with metaphysical cycles. The stone can clearly open and activate the Third Eye chakra and bring the connection to the higher rooms. Its tuna can clear blockages from all the chakras and activate underline all the chakras and connect the hearts to the chakra. If you place this stone on your third eye chakra, it will help to perfect its functioning and give you more vivid dreams, deeper meaning to life and increase the creation and spiritual awakening.

By carrying the stone, it will keep you open to new perceptions. This stone helps to enhance the flow of energy between the heart and the third eye and bridge the gap between intellectual and emotional understanding. It also allows you to live from your heart moldavite, which can often help it to work quickly and intensely. You must make sure that you are ready for a change when you're working with this stone.

Oolite

The eight stone is called is Oolite. This is a wonderful tool for working with the third eye as it helps to increase your inner vision. Oolite is known for its ability to clearly open and activate the Third Eye chakra. These gentle crystals can help you better recognize the patterns in life and helps you to release any control issues that can be placed directly on the third eye during meditation to open up psychic abilities and enhance self-trust. It can help to bring greater mental clarity on any subject and can be helpful for anyone who is going through a learning process. Physically, this stone can stimulate detoxification and improves healing in the liver.

Herkimer Diamond

The 9-th one is a Herkimer Diamond. The stone is another common third Eye chakra stone that is often used to enhance inner vision. The stone works with the third eye chakra and also the Crown chakra and create a bridge between these two chakras so that you will better understand the Divine purpose behind any intuitive inside. The stone can enhance meditative state, memory function, and visualization, and also help to bring a higher level of awareness to you. This tune is a great meditation to and helps to bring you to the highest vibration level possible while still remaining within the physical body. It helps to connect the physical, astral planes and facilitate astral travel.

Unakite

The 10-th stone is Unakite. This stone is unitary and can help to collect information and receive from the third Eye into the root chakra. This is a very helpful stone for meditation experiences that we usually forget as soon as we finish the medication. Unakite can also work in reverse, in the form of emotional therapy and pull repressed feelings up from your root chakra so that you'll be able to understand it. The stone works with the heart chakra so that you better understand the relation between the events in life and the natural order of the universe. The stone unites the root heart and Third Eye chakra. It is also good for lucid dreaming and astral travel.

Indigo Aura

The 11-th one is called Indigo aura. This stone is also known as Cancer Nura, and it is created when a clear quart is placed in a vacuum and infused with vaporized golden indigo. The stone has a unique vibration that is very good for meditation and healing Houston. It can help you raise your vibrations. The stone also works with all the copper chakras and helps to maintain a strong connection between them so that energy and transformation will be passed through them. Most of the stones also facilitate the release of chronic negativity and protect and balance your third eye in the process.

The stone is good for the quest of awakening your third eye. Although different colorful crystals can open the third eye, you can use gemstones and crystals in the purple indigo and violet color palette. This color palette helps to awaken balance and the Third Eye. So, place the neutral and gemstone slightly above your head, high during meditation. Once you begin to work with this stone, you will start receiving guidance messages and visions from it. Always try to have the courage to follow through on what your intuition is offering you.

Chapter 14: Avoid Using Electronics

Funny I would be saying "Avoid using electronics" this being an eBook and all. But, it is a not brainer that we as a culture are constantly using electronic devices to gain the latest news, talk to friends, or alleviate boredom. However, using electronics can greatly impact the ability for your Pineal Gland to work its magic. This is because the radio waves given off by electronics may interfere with the messages being sent inside of your brain thus messing up the levels of melatonin excreted in the brain. Therefore lessening your usage of electronics will definitely help how successfully you achieve your third eye. Make sure that if you do decide to continue using electronics that you halt the usage of them at least an hour before you go to sleep otherwise your REM cycle will become disorderly. Because REM is the time during the day where melatonin levels are at an all time high, you do not want to do anything that might ruin the chance of opening your third eye. Instead of using electronics a person may choose to meditate more to further increase the Pineal Gland production of endocrine. There are many activities that a person may choose to do instead of using their electronic devices, such as doing a sport or reading a book on how to further your spiritual awakening.

Chapter 15: Crystals And Health

Up until now, you have been given information about how crystals are associated with different aspects of your life. In this section, you will learn about the different ways in which you can use crystals to improve your health.

Insomnia

Insomnia can be quite problematic. Don't you feel quite tired and cranky when you don't get a good night's sleep? Imagine being unable to sleep for many nights in a row. Crystals can certainly be used to tackle insomnia. However, the crystal that you use will depend on the cause of your insomnia. Insomnia can be caused by a variety of reasons. So, you might have to experiment a little with different crystals to find one that works well for you. Insomnia can be caused by tension or stress. It can also be caused by any health issues or even occur because of negative thoughts.

If you want to relieve stress and tackle insomnia, you can use crystals like amethyst, rose quartz, and citrine. By wearing these crystals or even keeping them close to your bed you can help improve the quality of your sleep. If insomnia is caused by negative thinking, then you can try using smoky quartz, tourmaline, or labradorite. You can place these crystals at the base of your bed or under your pillow to get restful sleep at night.

Lack of energy

As mentioned in the previous section, the different colors that can help increase energy are red, yellow, and orange. So, by using crystals of these bright colors, you can help increase your energy levels. If you want to feel more energized, then you can use golden amber, topaz, or ruby. If you want to increase your motivation levels, then you can use jasper, tiger's eye, or dark citrine. Holding these crystals close to your solar plexus can help increase your energy levels. To make this doubly effective, you can combine these crystals with clear quartz.

Headache

Headaches can be caused by a variety of reasons. They can be caused from overthinking, an imbalance in energy, a lack of sleep, tension, or even negative thoughts. If the headache is caused by tension, you can use stones like amethyst, turquoise, or amber. You can also use blue-colored stones to relieve yourself of any headache. Any imbalance in the energy of the solar chakra can also cause headaches. So, by addressing the issue you can successfully get rid of the headaches you are facing.

Problems with libido

All sexual feelings are associated with the sacral chakra. Any imbalance of energies in this chakra can cause issues with libido. Also, the lack of any sexual feelings can be because of emotional imbalances too. If emotions are the reason why your sexual energy is blocked, then you can use crystals like fluorite or red garnet.

Difficulty in concentrating

Quartz can help bring about clarity of mind whereas Carnelian can help in keeping any unwanted thoughts away from you. Focus and concentration can be improved by using quartz. Lapis lazuli, amethyst, amber, and citrine are associated with the throat and third-eye chakras. Any imbalance in these chakras can make it rather difficult to concentrate or focus. Addressing the energy blockages in these chakras by using the appropriate crystals, you can help improve your mental clarity. Once you have mental clarity, it becomes easier to concentrate.

You will learn more about the ways in which you can heal and balance the energies of each of these chakras in the subsequent chapters. Now that you know how helpful crystals are, it is time to learn about the different types of crystals.

Benefits of activating the pineal gland

Activation of this gland in antiquity, according to his deep knowledge of health and life, the shamans were almost gods that could cure either mild diseases including cancers, depression, phobias. And that cured all kinds of diseases to the community. But humanity as a whole lost all that rich information,

What can cure Activating the Pineal Gland? Cure diseases, traumas, activate the imagination, ultimately to use more of our own energy. People from all over the world using the Energy Method pineal gland reported spontaneous healings.

- Depression
- Cancer
- Anorexia
- Diabetes
- Kidney Problems
- Arthritis
- Tobacco
- Colon Irritable
- Insomnia

Chapter 16: The Sixth Sense

While we are most all aware of the five senses normal to humans (sight, smell, taste, touch and hearing), many do not fully understand what the sixth sense actually means.

Have you ever heard of people who seem to know something will happen before it does? Have a gut feeling they are supposed to do something only to be proven it true? This is the sixth sense, a way in which a body can tell something that the other five senses cannot.

Telepathy is a form of the sixth sense. This is where one person is able to share their thoughts with another or perhaps read another's thoughts but is not within close proximity. Comics spoof this phenomenon as often as real people with the gift perform in front of audiences. Like any other facet of the subject, it is highly controversial with the adamant believers and non-believers holding their ground.

ESP (Extrasensory Perception) has enabled clairvoyants to make astonishing but truthful statements. For instance, the fire in Sweden in 1759 that Emmanuel Swedenborg proclaimed was occurring near his home 300 miles from where he was attending a party.

The sixth sense has been intensely studied by the scientific community for decades upon decades. It was thought at one time that perhaps ESP was stronger when people were resting or asleep. Sleep laboratories had a person sleeping in one room while in another a volunteer stared at a photo. There were many of the sleepers who claimed to have dreams that involved the picture being stared at in the other room.

Another form of the sixth sense can be seen with out of body experiences (OBE). When a person faces a near death experience, or perhaps does technically die for a short amount of time before being brought back, they can sometimes describe what is known as an out of body experience. There are many other types of OBE's, such as astral projection or travel. Some are spontaneous, such as dreaming or near death, while others can be induced such as with meditation or chemically. These OBE's are related to the third eye in that these experiences involve a separate plane of existence that the third eye also allows us to travel through.

Some scientists believe that when one sense is unavailable, the others become stronger. This can be evidenced by a blind person having an acute sense of hearing for example. Theoretically the sixth sense could be included in this concept. Charles Honorton in the 1970's started testing this idea and it is still a working theory today. Honorton used a test developed by Wolfgang Metzger called the ganzfeld experiment. The test uses sensory deprivation in order to bring out the ESP of the subject. The findings from this experiment are the subject of a long and heated debate as to whether or not they are random results or if they can be considered conclusive evidence.

Part of the New Age of thinking involves the Law of Attraction. This is the idea that like thinking will bring about like action. For example if you meditate and envision yourself as gaining wealth and you concentrate on that idea hard enough, money will be "attracted" or end up in your life. Theoretically this can be used in conjunction with opening the third eye in order to put your concentration on such items into another plane of existence. You could also use the law of attraction to assist in opening the third eye. By visualizing yourself awakening the eye, this could bring you into touch with your third eye faster.

In order to assist with using the Law of Attraction it is important to clear your mind of any doubts you have about the goal you are setting. Continuing with the previous example, if you are envisioning yourself as wealthy, but you have a small doubt in the back of your mind that you do not deserve such wealth, then you are blocking yourself before you even begin. In order to have a successful experience you must use meditation in order to purge such contradictory thoughts from your mind.

Chapter 17: Using Yoga to Enhance the Power of Your 3rd Eye

Do you need the working of your third eye being consistently optimal or fluctuating at will? Of course whatever makes you enlightened, relaxed and happy had better remain working well at all times. Unfortunately, there are lots of things that happen around you that are a threat to the good working of your third eye. You may possibly be aware, for instance, that negative thinking can blur your vision from the perspective of your third eye. Being fearful is another factor. And there are lots more of those apparently trivial things that can turn you to an ordinary Joe who does not see beyond the physical things that are within view of ordinary sight.

Fortunately, there are other helpful ways beyond what has already been mentioned in this book that can have your sixth chakra well balanced. Yes, well balanced, because it is when your 6th chakra is well aligned and facilitating great flow of energy that you feel great, intuitive and free. And that is how you get to know things beyond the ordinary folk whose 3rd eye is just but a little crack on the pineal gland.

How Yoga enhances the working of your 3rd Eye

Any idea what yoga is? Well, different people may have different ways of explaining it, but the long and short of it is that it is a kind of science whose practice began ages ago, which gets you into a tranquil state where you know no turbulence of thought nor any physical restlessness. At that moment, it is like everything is still. You are just in a quiet and serene state. You are not thinking about the future, analyzing your past or even worrying about the present – you just are.

Now what is the essence of just being? Good question – it is in just being that you get to the heightened level of self awareness. And in this state, you are one happy human being. Ever heard of that verse in the Christian Holy Book, the Bible, which says be still and you will know that I'm God? Well, that is a spiritual angle to stillness and quietude. And you know the level of awareness you are looking to achieve by opening your third eye is one that is spiritual. It is that awareness that adds great meaning to your life so that you are no longer afraid of the brevity of your physical life.

So in yoga, what you do is stop focusing on outward influences to direct your thinking. Instead, you direct your energy inwards to your mind, where you let that intense energy enhance your consciousness.

Again, why is it important that your third eye is open? Simple:

- You want to see beyond the physical
- You want better perception of things and situations

- You want to have high intuition
- You would like to enjoy great dreams
- You would like to have great visions
- You want to have great imagination
- You want to be highly inspired
- You want that guidance that comes from within you
- You want to be able to link the physical and spiritual worlds in a harmonious way.
- You want to visualize your existence in totality – every aspect of your life being an integral part of your life as a whole.

It will help you to know that in the case of opening or enhancing your third eye, some yoga poses are most preferable.

Thunderbolt pose – Vajrasana

The term's first part, **Vajra**, bears the meaning of thunderbolt, while the second part, **asana**, is a particular posture that you sit in while performing some form of yoga – actually the **hatha** yoga. Vajra is actually god's own weapon – god Indra, who is heaven's ruler.

In this thunderbolt post, you get your body purified, in preparation for meditation. And generally when doing **hatha** yoga, you develop a good level of awareness and also control over your body's internal state.

How does the thunderbolt pose help?

Plenty:

- It tones down your personal criticism; that inner critic that causes you to judge yourself harshly leading you to feel terrible about yourself.
- It creates a great observer of you

What this essentially means is that you are able to look at your thoughts without being emotionally affected by them. So it is not like someone is asking you to assume you have no thoughts – no. But how you handle those thoughts is what is important to the working of your third eye. So you are observing your thoughts with strictly no engagement with them.

Still, make no mistake about this state of observation. Although those thoughts do not influence you, the impact you have on them from sheer observation is significant. Of course you will be observing them with your intense energy, and so inevitably, you are going to impact them; and that is in a good way. That is the reason the outcome of this thunderbolt pose is you feeling whole again.

How to form the thunderbolt pose:

- Sit down. How?

- Well – you sit on your own heels and with your knees apart
- In the meantime, you have your spine straight

Feeling a bit uncomfortable, particularly your knees? No problem – a towel beneath your butt will do

- Handle your palms well. How?
- By placing them right on your thighs
- Try not to strain your spine. How?
- By releasing your entire weight downwards through your seat bones
- Now inhale deep through your nose and then exhale in a similar fashion
- Allow your spine to have a feel of its full length upwards
- Release your shoulders so that they feel no tension
- At the same time, let your shoulders spread wide
- Adjust your gaze. How? Easy:
- In front of you. How far? Say, about a stretch of 1.2 meters

- And mind your focus – should be on the floor; or down on the ground
- In your pose, let your deep inhaling and exhaling continue

- And continue to observe your thoughts.

In your quietude and pose, you will notice your thoughts moving along like clouds passing through a sky lit by the glow of a sunny day. The important thing for you is to remember – just observing; no engaging, as far as those thoughts are concerned.

Can you now see what you will effectively be doing? You will be relaxing your body as well as your mind as you play the detached observer.

And what are the benefits of this form of yoga?

- You will find yourself being more compassionate with yourself
- You will be able to identify behavior patterns that are not helpful to you
- You will be in a position to design the changes necessary for those awful behavior patterns for your own good
- You will feel in harmony with other people in your life and with those around you
- You will practically experience relatively much more peace than before
- You will feel even more knowledgeable deep within you
- You will experience increased joy

Downward Facing Dog – Adho Mukha Svanasana

This is one pose that prepares you for a headstand. A headstand is bound to increase the flow of blood into your head, and so this pose is meant to help you handle that. In this Downward Facing Dog pose, ensure your focus is on your third eye.

- This is how you form the pose:
- Use the floor where you are standing on for kneeling.
- Spread a mat on the floor on which you will have a grip as you do your yoga pose
- While in a kneeling position, go on your fours with your back straight out; that is, flat.
- Stretch your good hands forwards a little more, and let your fingers spread out. In fact, not just the fingers – even your palms need to be spread out flat. Generally your hands should be firm on the ground.
- Now the moves:
- Prepare to exhale. As you exhale, straighten out your legs
- And your feet need to be steady and flat on the floor even at that time

- In the meantime, your tailbone is being lifted upwards
- You also need to keep lifting your seat bones to the direction of the ceiling
- And your tailbone, meanwhile, is kind of pulling away from your pelvis

- Make your knees feel strong ensuring they do not get locked
- Essentially, in the Adho Mukha Svanasana pose, your arms are straightened out; your hands open and spread out on the mat; with your palms well pressed on the mat.

How long is the recommended time to remain in this Downward Facing Dog yoga pose?

Well, one to three minutes make the ideal duration.

And how precisely do you benefit?

- Your mind calms down
- Your entire body gets energized

Chapter 18: Yoga

Yoga, the act of adopting certain purposeful poses, is believed to activate the chakras. The third eye chakra is no exception. The simple poses described in this chapter are the preferred movements of many of the world's most altruistic yogis. Provided that you are physically capable, consider practicing yoga as a method for awakening your third eye and its psychic capabilities.

Child Pose

The simplest of yoga poses, the child pose puts its adopters in resting states that stretch the joints on the lower half of the body. In addition, the pose aids in the elimination of exhaustion and stress. The forward-leaning nature of this pose places a pressure on and therefore activates the third eye and its corresponding chakra.

To perform this pose, start by sitting on your knees. Then, point the heels of your feet outwards, keeping your knees hip-length apart. You should end up sitting on your feet. Next, stretch forward and touch the center of your forehead to the ground. Place your arms outstretched in front of your head with your palms facing downwards. Thoroughly exhale. Then, while inhaling, move your arms towards your rear until they lie on the ground parallel with your bent legs. Your palms should face the sky. Exhale and continually repeat the motions until you feel satisfied with the results.

Eagle Pose

More difficult than the child pose, this yoga pose necessitates balance. While intently concentrating on keeping your physical balance, your third eye will balance out in response.

First, stand on your feet, keeping them the same distance apart as your shoulders are from one another. Do not lock your knees; keep them subtly bent. Next, raise your left foot and lay the thigh on the left side of your body across your right thigh. Your right foot should be holding you up at this point. Aim the toes on your left foot at the ground. Then, lower that same foot and bring it around your right leg so that you can hook your left foot's top onto your right leg's calf. Using the right foot for balance, extend your arms out so that they end up parallel with the ground. Next, keeping them extended, intersect your arms in front of your torso in such a way that leaves your right arm on top of your left. Now bend your arms at the elbows. Your left elbow's crook should contain the point of your right elbow if you have followed the method correctly up to this point.

Without adjusting the rest of your body parts, lift your forearms so that they become perpendicular to the ground. You should end up with the backs of your hands aligned towards one another. Next, shift your hands so that your palms face on another–move your right hand to the right and left hand left; in other words, uncross your arms. Finally, touch your palms against one another, applying gentle pressure. Extend your arms and fingertips upwards at the sky. Maintain this pose for fifteen to thirty seconds and, when you are ready, return to a neutral standing position.

Repeat this process with the opposite sides of the body.

The eagle pose will help balance out your third eye. As you practice developing your physical balance, your third eye will follow suit. Yogis around the world teach this pose as part of their courses.

Uttanasana

Also known as the standing forward bend, this pose will tap into the third eye's energy reserves and strengthen the relaxing feeling that an activated third eye brings about. It works by directing the body's natural blood flow towards the brain, the region of the body responsible for housing the third eye. In turn, the third eye gets blessed with an increase in blood flow, activating the appendage in the process.

To begin, stand in a comfortable position. Next, while inhaling, extend your arms skywards towards the ceiling. Then, while exhaling, start to lean over at the hips, moving your hands downwards to your sides with your palms aimed at the ground. Keep bending over, lowering one vertebra at a time. From the start, you should intend to touch your forehead to your shins. It is perfectly fine if you are unable to do so, but keeping that intention in mind will help you make the proper movements.

Once you are fully bent over with your spine fully extended, wrap your hands around the backs of your ankles, locking your fingers for extra support. Keep your knees as straight as you possibly can. If possible, rest your head against either your kneecaps or shins, depending on your body type and the extent of your flexibility. Lastly, while inhaling, raise yourself back into a standing position one vertebra at a time.

Inverting your head in this fashion will send to the head the needed blood supply to activate the third eye.

Dolphin Pose

This pose aims to stretch out the back, hamstrings, arms, and shoulders. As a result, it is designed to invoke balance in those who adopt it. As alluded to earlier, the third eye responds greatly to improvements in the physical sense of balance. In addition, adopting this pose will cause your blood flow to partially reverse, further delivering an increased amount of blood circulation to your brain and nearby face muscles. In effect, in addition to stimulating the third eye, this pose assists in the relief of headaches, hearing problems, vision issues, and stress.

To begin, start in the downward dog position with your soles and palms flat on the ground, arching your back in such a way that makes your buttocks your apex. Then, keeping your palms turned downwards, rest the entirety of your forearms on the ground so that your elbows touch the floor too. You want to have your shoulders aligned vertically with your elbows. Your feet should be kept the same distance apart from one another as are your hips.

Next, press your shoulder blades back towards your ribcage and move your shoulders in the opposite direction of your ears so that your neck is fully exposed. Put weight on your pelvis so that your heels do not come off of the floor. Fix your gaze on your choice of either the floor space either between your elbows, your feet, or somewhere in between. Inhale and breathe out five to seven times each without consciously moving.

During the time in which you hold this pose, direct your focus to your third eye. Giving it attention will help stimulate it.

Chapter 19: Other Practical Advice for Opening the Third Eye

The desire to open the third eye is a great place to start because it states your intention and your commitment to what you are doing. However, you will not get far by willing it to be open. You need focused, meditative practice and the ability to connect to the third eye as you go through your day. You are going to find that your third eye is not just open when you are actively trying to open it—but at all times as you go through life. The more you focus, the more active it will be. To give yourself the greatest chance of success, consider adopting some of these habits or taking these extra steps.

Meditate Through the Day (Not Just When You Are Trying to Activate the Third Eye)

Meditation is a major part of opening the third eye, especially when you are actively practicing. If you have never meditated before, it can be challenging to get yourself in the right mindset of focus and relaxation. Instead of diving into meditation while trying to open the third eye, practice meditation beforehand.

People who live particularly busy or stressful lifestyles can struggle with meditation at first. Practice quieting your mind through the day. To fall into meditation, sit in a quiet area and focus on your breathing. If your mind wanders, choose a single thing to focus on. Imagine an apple or a tennis ball in your mind, down to the detail. Stare at that single object until it blurs out of focus. Do not think anything about it, just focus on your breathing and look at the object.

Over time, you will not need to visualize an object. You can focus on your breathing and hear your mind quiet, as the world around you melts away. Be proud even if you do this for a minute—the length will gradually increase the more that you practice.

Practice Mindfulness during Your Day-to-Day Activities

Think back to the last time you went out with family or friends. How many times did you check your phone? How many times did someone repeat themselves because you spaced out or were not genuinely listening to what they were saying? Now, consider how you do housework or travel on your way to work. Do you notice the way that the muscles in your arm move as you scrub dishes or really see your surroundings while you commute to work? What about your free time? Do you take showers just to get clean, or do you notice the way that the water feels as it runs down your body?

When you make it a practice to immerse yourself in your surroundings, you will find greater fulfillment in life. Being mindful is not a simple practice—it is a lifestyle. It helps you learn to immerse yourself into your surroundings and fully experience everything that you do. How many times a day do you let your mind wander? Do you

143

find yourself seeing the surroundings as you drive, or thinking about the day ahead of you? When you walk your dog, are you on the phone checking your emails or enjoying the feeling of the pavement under your feet and the happy panting of your dog? Most people go into this autopilot mode, where they do not really experience what they are doing. This leads to feelings of dissatisfaction and takes you away from the experience that is living life.

Instead of following your typical routine, make it a habit to consciously immerse yourself in what you are doing. Feel the way your muscles move when you write, type, or do chores. Pay attention to your heartbeat when you are taking a walk and the scenery as you drive in your car. If you are having trouble switching out of autopilot, switch up your routine. Start walking your dog in the mornings instead of at night or take a different route to work. Switching up your routine will stop that autopilot mode.

You must also make it a conscious habit of reminding yourself not to let your mind wander. Remind yourself when your thoughts wander that thinking aimlessly is not your goal right now. You should not be problem-solving, stressing about the day, or thinking about what you must do when you finish meditating. Do not judge your thoughts or question them, but also let them go.

Reinforce Third Eye Connections

Things like connectedness to the energy flow of the life around you and greater connectedness to the creative part of the brain are both caused by activation of the third eye. It makes sense, therefore, that you can increase your connectedness to the third eye by doing creative activities or being out in nature when you can truly feel the connection to all that is around you.

Being mindful can help you tune in to the energy that is all around you, regardless of what you are doing. This is especially true out in nature. Find time to walk in the woods or visit a pond and feel the presence of life there. Listen to the rustles of squirrels and other woodland critters and the songs of birds. Hear the songs of a bullfrog at the pond and the splash of fish as they jump around. Go to the dog park and watch how the dogs run and play with the kids and people there, while the grass trembles beneath their feet and the butterflies dance in the bushes. Looking up at the night sky can also foster this sense of connectedness and give you a perspective of your small, but significant role in the energy that exists in the universe.

Creativity also breaks the boundaries of the rational mind and helps you open to the possibilities. The thing about creativity is that it does not have to be something complicated—start small. Start coloring in your free time or listen to music that you wouldn't normally. What this does is open the channel of your mind, giving you a greater capacity to unfold the logical boundaries that have kept you from activating your third eye previously.

Practice Grounding

Grounding is another useful technique that can help bring you to a center of peace and calm and set the right environment for opening the third eye. The practice of grounding involves planting yourself firmly as one with the earth. Often, sitting on the ground or standing while barefoot is helpful, especially if you have direct contact with the earth. Deep breathe as if you were meditating and relax your mind. Then, feel the sensation of a tree growing from you, with the roots coming out of your feet or down your spine and traveling deep into the earth, where they root you and hold you steady. This can help you create a center of focus once you are ready to attempt to open the third eye.

Grounding is essential to the flow of energy through your body. When you are grounded, energy is going to flow uninhibited through and from your chakras. It gives you a foundation to build on. As you find your center and ground yourself, you are securing yourself at the foundation, so you have the mindset that you need to soar.

Advice on Choosing a Teacher

When you learn about opening the third eye from someone else, you will feel a deeper sense of connection to their energies. It can be useful to have someone guide you through the process of opening the third eye, especially if you are having difficulty focusing or are unsure if you are using the right techniques. Working with a teacher gives you a type of guided practice, as well as reassurance that it is possible to connect to the third eye.

There are a lot of factors that go into choosing a teacher. It is important to remember that whoever you decide to work with should match your own energy and make it easier to reach your third eye, not more difficult. Think back to the chapter on natures and what you may want to accomplish with the third eye. Keep in mind that the experience you will have with a teacher depends heavily on if your natures are aligned. Having the same goal can strengthen the connection and make it easier for you to activate the third eye.

Unfortunately, the problem with using a teacher to help you awaken the third eye is that teachers are not easy to find. You are not going to flip through the pages of a phone book or other directory and find someone who is authentically connected to the third eye. Many of the psychics that exist there are not truly connected with their third eye, but instead, rely on contextual clues and other hints to help them divulge information about other people.

Be wary of teachers that use their ego to define their ability. Part of being connected to the third eye is being connected with the heavens, earth, and flow of energy through all that exists. Someone who is authentically connected with their third eye is not going to brag about their abilities or make your promises about what you can accomplish together. Something else to keep in mind is that an authentic third eye teacher may be difficult to find. Most of these practitioners do not work as psychics or in other mystical lines of work. They use their third eye abilities to improve their life along with the lives of those around them, but often do not reveal their abilities to strangers because not everyone is receptive or understanding of the third eye's energy. Though someone, who has achieved a high level of activation of their third eye, will not lose their abilities just because someone casts a shadow of doubt over their abilities, but the negative energy can still have mild effects. Additionally, it is not uncommon for people to judge those who have developed extra abilities. Because of their connection to the third eye, they are often judged and grouped with the 'frauds' that exist in the world.

Know How to Close the Third Eye

Have you ever been 'trapped' in a bad dream? You may have experienced great sadness or fear but found yourself frozen instead of waking up. As the third eye is connected to the dream world and has the power to connect you with other planes, it is essential that you have the skill to close off the third eye when you become overwhelmed.

Keep in mind that the third eye does not have an eyelid. Closing the connection is not going to be as simple as covering it with an eyelid. Also, keep in mind that once you have opened it, that connection is always going to exist. The 'closing' that is spoken of, therefore, is learning to manage the senses of the third eye or at the very least training your mind to ignore what has been presented in front of you.

Mantras

As mantras are commonly used to open the third eye, they can also be used to guide its sight or close it when necessary. People who are overwhelmed by their senses or who see unwanted visions often find themselves afraid of opening the third eye. It is important not to let this fear overcome you. Instead, focus on a mantra to help dispel darkness. This will bring your journey with the third eye into the light, creating a more positive experience.

One of the reasons that people tend to shy away from mantras is because of pronunciation. Many of them are rooted in Sanskrit or other languages. However, keep in mind that as with any language, pronouncing the mantra properly will come easier with time. What matters most is the intention behind what you are saying and what you believe to be true. Pronunciation can help too, however, so if you cannot connect with a teacher then finding videos of people saying the mantras can help.

Kala Bhairava

The Kala Bhairava mantra is one that comes from Hawaiian practices. The meaning translates into English as:

- Kala- Dark times
- Bhai- Fear
- Rava- Destroyer

According to Hawaiian tradition, Kala Bhairava manifests as Lord Shiva and destroys darkness and fear. It does this by bringing light into the situation and breaking up the darkness with the same light.

Mantras are something that must be practiced, even before you have a dark encounter. Even something like saying the mantra quietly throughout the day can prepare you for when you open your third eye. Each time that you repeat Kala Bhairava, you will experience the feeling of light and peace in your soul.

Warning about Closing the Third Eye

Be aware that as you close the third eye, you are training your mind to ignore any visions or experiences that you are having. This becomes second nature with time—as you trained your mind to be receptive to the third eye, you can also train your mind to skip past anything you are seeing.

To keep the eye closed permanently, remember that judgment will hinder the opening of the third eye. You will shut down the potential of the third eye if you judge it or if you take in the judgmental

154

opinions of the people around you. Tell yourself that the third eye is an impossible phenomenon and that the things you are seeing are just your mind playing tricks on you. This will make the third eye disappear rapidly—but it will be very hard to open it again if you teach your mind that it is not possible. Be sure this is what you want before judging the third eye in a way that eliminates your abilities entirely.

Chapter 20: Realigning Your Energy

Knowing where your energy is blocked is the key to fixing it. Energy is constantly moving and changing, and any chakra could be misaligned at any given time. The result is an imbalanced life, and the symptoms of that can be pretty obvious if you look.

Being conscious and vigilant of the subtle cues your body and mind give you is a great way to tell if your chakras are aligned. For example, if you are suddenly developing indigestion with foods that have never given you a problem, your solar plexus chakra may be out of line.

It is important to know how to manipulate the energy of each chakra to realign and bring new energy to the area. Take a look at each individual chakra to find out how to keep it in line. You will notice that exercise in general, along with specifically targeted exercise can help align chakras, as well as a good diet.

Root chakra: Using essential oils myrrh or cedarwood in the methods described in chapter 3 can help draw energy to this chakra. Exercises that root the feet firmly to the ground, like jogging or walking, and yoga poses like warrior can help as well.

Sacral chakra: Use the scent of jasmine to invigorate this chakra. Any exercise that works the abdominal muscles will stimulate energy in this area as well. Try warrior and other yoga poses that draw heat to the body.

Solar plexus chakra: Ginger and lemon tea can really help soothe this chakra. These elements have been recommended for ages to help with general indigestion.

Turns out, they have been realigning your solar plexus all along. As with the sacral chakra, abdominal exercises also draw energy to this chakra.

Heart chakra: Practicing conscious self-love and compassion for others is the best way to realign your heart chakra. If you are feeling disconnected from others, make the first move and get involved with people.

Exercises that stretch the chest cavity can help open up your heart chakra. Try cobra in yoga, or simply meet your hands behind your back and open the area. Essential oils like peppermint and thyme help open the respiratory system and are especially helpful if you are dealing with mucus or infection.

Throat chakra: Playing on the idea of opening up air passages, eucalyptus and peppermint oils are great to clear the throat chakra as well. Use honey and lemon to soothe a sore throat, and do exercises that loosen the shoulders and neck. In yoga, do neck rolls or downward dog to release tension in the region.

Third eye chakra: As we touched on earlier, using healing crystals that are indigo can help redirect energy in the third eye. In addition, strong scents like sage help awaken your senses and restore energy to the mind and third eye. Yoga poses that focus on the forehead to the ground, like child's pose, will also be beneficial. Don't forget about meditation as well. More on that later.

Crown chakra: Since this is the chakra that is partially responsible for energy within all of the chakras, it is vital to keep this one healthy. Floral and citrus scents tend to awaken this chakra. It also helps being outside, as you can then take in a greater amount of energy from sunlight. Get in better touch with your inner spirit by being connected with nature.

Life is about juggling all of your responsibilities with joy and relaxation. If you focus too much on one aspect of your life, others will suffer. For example, if you are very focused on your career, your relationships will likely suffer, simply for lack of time.

A great practice to start doing every day is taking stock of the important parts of your life. Make a list of four or five major important areas of your life. For example, these could be your family, friends, career, and money (a form of security). Each and every day, take stock of what you have focused on most. Likely, this means that another one of your important categories has been generally neglected.

Make adjustments to bring some balance to that system. If you were forced to work all day, make sure to spend some time with the kids and connect with them when you get home.

The course of your energy depends on where you put your focus. Energy flows where the mind goes. If you focus your attention on one thing, and one thing only, a great deal of energy will flow there to support it. This also means that energy is being taken away from something else, as a law of physics. It is human nature to become transfixed with things, and it is difficult to maintain good balance. Make a conscious effort to pull your mind back into balance for the sake of your overall well-being.

The quality of the energy around you will also have a major impact on your well being and emotional health. If you are surrounded by positive influences and people with your best interests in mind, it will be very easy to be emotionally well, as you are accepting positive energy from your environment.

More likely than not, you are exposed to negative energy throughout the day. It could be related to a strained relationship, a difficult job, or just general bad vibes wherever you go. In your time on this planet, you may have noticed that a select few people always seem to be afflicted with problems and unfortunate circumstances. For example, their car always seems to be broken, they carry on dramatic relationships, and things never seem to work out in their favor.

There is a reason for that. Some people attract only negative energy because they exude negative energy. You get back what you put out there, the well-known rule of karma. Being callous, uncaring and down on yourself only brings about the same old thing. While it is impossible to avoid negativity completely, it is certainly possible to change your circumstances by altering what type of energy you put out there.

The point is, the unfortunate events happening in your life are not the universe 'punishing you,' it is you punishing yourself with your own internal negativity. Changing your thoughts and actions to be more positive can cause a dramatic shift in the course of your life. You have the power to consciously change how you feel about certain events, and how you react to negativity. Doing so blocks that negativity from entering your space. Positivity always wins over negativity.

Remember too that we are mobile creatures, not trees that are destined to grow in the same spot forever. If you do not like the energy around you and the circumstances you are planted in, simply move yourself out of it. This may mean ending volatile relationships, changing jobs, or even uprooting your life completely. It is your right and responsibility to take yourself out of the negativity. Failing to do so will continue to cause negative events in your life. Do you want to be responsible for your own demise?

Chapter 21: The Religious Links of the Third Eye

The term "third eye" or "inner eye" carries different meanings in different faiths/religions of the world. In the metaphysical science it refers to enlightenment and the ability to exercise psychic powers. Although this term may carry different meanings in different faiths of the world, it always relates back to the ability to see the unseen and provide perception beyond the ordinary sight. It refers to the gate that leads to the spiritual realms and take you to the higher levels of consciousness. In the world of religions, those who possess an activated third eye are termed as seers and are always given high regards. In the theosophical world this term relates to the pineal glands.

Let us have a look at some of the religions of the world and find out the meaning of the Third eye.

Hindu and Buddhist Religions

Out of all the religions of the world, the term "third eye" carries the most importance in the Buddhist and Hindu religions. These religions treat the third eye as the symbol of wisdom and enlightenment. In the Hindu religion you will find many people wear a "tilka" a small dot on their forehead exactly where the third eye is located, just to highlight the importance of third eye and benefit from it. Their Gods namely Buddha and Shiva are depicted with a third eye image.

Third Eye in Christianity

There are no strong evidences of third eye in the Christian faith, as most of the teaching and Holy Books in the Christian faith enforce that all the spiritual lights, senses, leadings, directions and communications come only from God by performing prayers and revelation from His words.

In Islam

In Islam the third eye refers to the phenomenon known as "wijdan" a state of mind in which a person is able to see in the spiritual world. The third eye is also referred to as the "eye of the heart" or more specifically "Chashm-e-Qalb" where Chashm means eye and Qalb mean heart. Muslims believe that when a person dies, he/she is removed from this material world and it taken to the spiritual world. There is no way to see the spiritual world unless you have that spiritual eye. Muslims strongly believe that this spiritual eye is only bestowed upon the righteous and chosen ones, the saints and the prophets.

Chapter 22: Practice Mindfulness Meditation

"Live the actual moment. Only this actual moment is life."

- THICH NHAT HANH

Mindfulness is an all-natural quality, which we all possess. It's the basic human ability to be fully present, aware of where we are and what we're doing, and not overly reactive or overwhelmed by what's happening around us. It is available to all of us at every moment, when we take the time to consciously practice it and to enjoy it. When you exercise mindfulness, you are practicing the ability to create time in yourself - time to think, to breathe, time between what happens to you and how you react to it.

How to Practice Mindfulness

While mindfulness may seem a simple task, it is not necessarily that easy. The actual work is in always making time each day to perform it. Here is a short exercise to get started with:

Take it easy. Find a quiet location to sit where you can feel calm and relaxed.

Set a period limit. If you're only starting, it can help to select a short time of, for example, 5 to 10 minutes.

Observe your body. You can sit in a chair with your feet on the floor, you can sit loosely cross-legged, in lotus posture, you can kneel - all these are acceptable positions. Just make sure you feel comfortable in a position you can stay in for a while.

Feel your breath. Focus your attention on every single breathing, every inhale and exhale. Your eyes may be opened or closed, but you may find it easier to maintain your focus if you keep your eyes closed; that way you'll block any unwanted distraction.

Take notice when your mind is wandering. Inevitably, your focus will leave your breathing and wander around other subjects. When you're caught thinking about something else, don't judge yourself - simply get your attention back to your breathing and start where you left off.

Figure 24: Mindfulness is one of the keys to open your third eye.

Chapter 23: Mindfulness Meditation - Higher levels of consciousness

The higher the released energy flows, the greater the spiritual uplift the meditator feels. Fire sparks emanating from the mouth of the kundalini snake reach the hemispheres of the brain, stimulating them more and more to vigorous activity. The meditator begins to experience the deepest ecstasy, joy, and peace. It seems that the whole body is plunged into an ocean of happiness and bliss.

With the stimulation of the right hemisphere, hidden possibilities of extrasensory perception, such as clairvoyance, clairaudience, telepathy, providence, and so on, come to the surface. Consciousness begins to expand and go beyond its borders, opening up new dimensions of cosmic unity. The sense of self-identity begins to make quantum leaps into the ever-increasing orbits of the cosmic mind. This stage of comprehension of time and space is a reward to the adept for all his efforts.

Here are a few meditations that help rise to higher levels of consciousness and control internal energy.

Meditation on the Clouds of Light

Find a comfortable place to relax. Let your thoughts flow freely, come, and go; you are only an observer. Take a deep breath, hold your breath. Check for tension in the body. If you find such areas, free them - and on the exhale to get rid of everything that prevents you from completely relaxing. Take a deep breath again. As you exhale, release all energy and all your thoughts from the body. Take a deep breath. Feel new energy entering the body; you breathe in new possibilities and allow the body to become light. Relax more and more - until you stop feeling the body.

When fully relaxed, imagine a colorful mist vibrating around you. You, being light, smoothly pass into this fog, just your being has a slightly higher density. Clouds of energy slowly float around you. Relax on one of them, feel safe. This cloud lifts you up and takes you to an infinite world. The boundaries between time and space are erased. You are immersed in a world of infinite beauty and endless possibilities. You are floating in the cloud, feeling how light you have become. Suddenly you see a giant rock below; the cloud softly and easily lands, you descend on a rock.

Feel the strength of the stone, feel the power emanating from the rock. You look back, and you see a big river. You cannot make out where it begins and where it ends. You are fascinated by the water stream. It is an endless river of energy, a river of life. You come closer to the water and try to examine its color, to feel it with your whole being. What sounds do you hear? You are the light, so you can safely enter the water, cross it, rush along with the stream, and when you want, stop.

Relax and try to realize what you need most at the moment. What is your main intention? What emotions will accompany you on the way to the chosen goal? Feel the energy of these emotions, feel how it moves through your light body, burns, pulsates. Inhale energy with your whole being. Try to see the paintings, images, symbols associated with it: they will appear in front of the inner eye themselves; you can only focus on them.

When you are completely filled with this energy, enter the river, dissolve for a moment in it, purify the energy, and then release it into the water. See how the energy cloud comes out of you, touches the water, and gradually disappears in the stream. Take a deep breath. Your desire merges with the source of life. Enjoy the river of life for some more time. Take a deep breath again and exit the river. Notice that the colored fog surrounds you again, and you rise up with it. You descend to the cloud and return. With each deep breath, you return to the outside world and feel peace and satisfaction.

Sacred Space Meditation

Relax, sit in a comfortable position. Close your eyes, calm your mind. Breathe slowly and deeply; breathing comes from the diaphragm. For a while, just breathe and pay attention to the spine. It is a pillar connecting earth and heaven.

Feel the energy being concentrated at both ends of this pillar. Let the flow of earthly energy move upward, exit the crown of the head, and disperse into the Universe. Together with the energy flow, all negative emotions, pain, anxiety, tension are carried away.

Your whole being is filled with peace. Let the mind be like the ocean, and thoughts -

bubbles appearing on the surface of the water. You may remember your thoughts better, but for now, remain a simple observer. Breathe deeper, gradually slow down your breathing. With each breath, relax your body and mind more and more.

Feel the cool red fog enveloping you. It is not hot, not cold: you can only feel it with your skin.

Feel yourself on a cloud firm enough to hold you on yourself, but very cozy and comfortable. Each part of your body rests on a cloud: legs, arms, back, neck, head - all organs feel calm. The cloud begins to plunge slowly into the red fog, and you plunge with it. Immersion is very slow; you go deeper and deeper and relax even more. The fog begins to change its color: from brilliant red to red-orange.

Gradually, the orange color changes to yellow-lemon. Your body is also painted in lemon color. You are floating on a cloud that carries you to the green summer lawn. You can even hear the wind shaking the grass, feel the flowing blue light from heaven.

Blue light turns into purple; moonless night comes, dark, peaceful, and quiet. The cloud you were floating on gently lands.

The fog disappears. You lie on your back on the green grass. You feel light blows of the wind; you can hear the faint chatter of night insects.

Wherever you are, there is always something that pulls you toward you. It may be someplace, person, impression. What you are thinking about may appear right next to you because you are in a sacred place of fulfillment of desires. Everything can change here, but any changes will occur only at your request. You built this place, inhabited it. Rise, explore the sacred space in which you are. May you meet with something (or about whom) have long dreamed of.

After a while, you will realize that the time has come to leave the sacred place. Say goodbye to what you saw, leave without regret, because you can always come back here whenever you want.

Lie on your back and again feel the fog enveloping you. This time it is dark, like a moonless sky. Feel the cloud again under your feet, arms, back, neck, and head. It supports you - and begins to rise very slowly.

Breathe deeply, watch the gradual change of colors: the dark color of the sky turns into blue, cyan, green, yellow. All this time, you continue to rise slowly; yellow turns to summer orange, then red. Let your mind still float, and your body will slowly return to the tangible world. You begin to feel the floor with your back, to realize the room in which you are. You are coming back.

Understanding the Benefits of a Strong Meditation Practice

The mindfulness movement is rapidly gaining popularity in the Western world. If before meditation was practiced only by people who are fond of various kinds of spiritual practices, now it is considered the most common thing. Now in Europe and here in the USA, the phrase "I practice meditation" no longer causes a wary-detached attitude, as before. So, what's the point? What are some of the benefits of meditation or mindfulness? Why are more and more people doing it? I will try to answer these questions in this chapter. But let's take it in order.

What Meditation Is

In 2007, a study was published that experimentally confirmed the previously existing hypothesis that a person has two different forms of self-consciousness, and different parts of the brain are responsible for them. These two forms of self-awareness are called the narrative mode (story mode, narrative mode of self-reference), and the experience mode (empirical mode, experiential mode of self-reference).

The narrative mode is a mechanism by which we can think about the past, present, and future. Its essence is that our

179

attention is partially or completely captured by thoughts that give meaning to what is happening. The story mode is responsible for our understanding of who we are, what is happening around us, what we are striving for, what connects us with others, and so on. The story mode connects the past, present, and future for us into one semantic picture.

The empirical mode is the ability to perceive our direct experience, what is happening to us at this second. Our direct experience consists of several parts. This is, firstly, the sensations realized with the help of the senses (hearing, sight, touch, smell, taste, balance). Secondly, these are internal sensations - thoughts, imagination, emotions, and internal states.

Meditation is the training of attention. When we meditate, we train to keep our focus on exactly what we are experiencing at the moment. That is, we train to be in the mode of experience.

Why Do We Need Each of These Forms of Self-Awareness?

Both forms of self-awareness are necessary. Narrative mode serves to perform any action. To do something, you need to make a decision. To make a decision, you need to somehow explain to yourself what is happening. Medicine knows cases of damage to the part of the brain that is responsible for the narrative regimen. In cases where this department completely loses its working capacity, a person turns into a vegetable. He does nothing more and does not say anything.

Once I read about one case when such a person fell into the pool and drowned. He could not have a motive to perform any actions for his salvation. For a motive to appear, one must first give the event some meaning. If the narrative mode does not work, what is happening seems pointless.

The empirical regime allows us to be in the present moment and feel what is happening to us. In addition to the fact that we get complete satisfaction from any pleasant sensations (for example, the pleasure of eating, music, sex, etc.), we are better aware of what is happening around us. That is, we can give the event meaning more accurately. The empirical mode allows us to adjust how we explain what is happening, taking into account what is happening here and now.

If the empirical regime is poorly trained, then our thoughts are more based on our ideas about ourselves and the world and to a lesser extent, on what is happening here and now.

Let's look at an example:

Victor works in sales. He is new to this business. He attended several trainings where he was told the theory. But he is not good at applying this theory in practice. When he speaks with the client, usually at some point, the client begins to close, and the contact disappears. Victor began to practice meditation. Now he notices that the contact disappears when he begins to feel excitement amid a desire to close the deal as soon as possible. Gradually, he began to recognize this sensation at an early stage and learned to behave more calmly, despite the excitement. Over time, he noticed that he began to feel more relaxed.

In this example, the practice of meditation helps Victor to pay attention to his feelings during a conversation with a client. This led to the fact that he understood the reason for the disappearance of contact with the client. As a result, over time, he first managed to adjust his behavior, and then his emotional reactions became adequate.

Awareness is a kind of feedback mechanism that allows you to adjust behavior. Without realizing what we feel, we usually act on autopilot.

Yet another example:

Andrew is a conflict person in terms of his personality. When he was angry, he could not stop. The conflict simply unwound according to a previously known scenario. But Andrew never thought about it. Each time he drew conclusions for himself and lived on. Conclusions usually came down to the fact that the other side is to blame.

When Andrew began to practice meditation, first of all, it helped him realize that he was behaving aggressively. Then he noticed that often in a conflict, he doesn't react to the essence of the issue, but to the form in which the other side answers him. This allowed him to react less emotionally. Andrew realized that from time to time, he spoke stingy, offensive phrases, the purpose of which was to offend another person. He began to learn to stop in time. The practice of mindfulness helps Andrew more often and faster turn off the autopilot in a conflict and do something for a peaceful resolution of the situation.

What Other Benefits Does Meditation Provide?

The fact is that the mechanisms of attention are the most low-level mechanisms of our consciousness. Therefore, the practice of meditation affects absolutely all aspects of our lives.

Known and research-confirmed effects include:

- Increased attention span. Reducing the number of random distractions.

- Improving self-control ability.

- Increasing the pain threshold.

- Improving learning and memorization.

- Reduces irritability and stress.

Meditation to Attain Your Divine Self

As you have seen in the mediation guides, the most common meditation technique is observing breathing. Even though it is very good for training concentration, in terms of awareness of your divine self, you need to take it up a notch. For this, I recommend trying a technique called marking or mental noting.

Marking is a technique from the attention category without a choice. In other words, we are not trying to concentrate on something specific, but simply try to notice what is happening to us, whatever that is.

And when we notice, we call it one word. Perhaps we feel some sensations in the body. Perhaps we are thinking about something. Maybe we want something. Maybe we imagine something. Anything. In a word.

There are various marking options without a choice. You can start with anyone. The easiest option is to use only three words: see, hear, and feel. Moreover, each word can refer to both external sensation and internal. For example, the word "hear" can denote perception by the hearing organs and the thought that "sounds" in the head.

As for the time for meditation, 10-15 minutes a day is enough to start. It is advisable to find the time when no one will bother you.

While meditating, you can sit, lie, stand, or walk. Eyes may be open or closed. You can sit on a chair or the floor. All this is not so important at first. It is important to remember that the practice of meditation is a long game. And therefore, at the first stage, it is advisable not to overdo it.

The practice of meditation is usually associated with people with Buddhist monasteries, where people come to live to someday achieve enlightenment. At the same time, enlightenment itself is usually not taken seriously but is used to denote a certain unattainable ideal that one will have to strive for a lifetime.

Probably, touching upon this topic, I may seem strange to some but still, take a chance. Enlightenment is an absolutely real and quite strong change in the work of the human psyche that can occur as a result of the practice of meditation. I know because it happened to me. It happens suddenly, at one point. In Buddhist texts, one can find descriptions of several stages of enlightenment. Each of these steps leads to a radical increase in the basic level of awareness.

Achieving enlightenment is no easy task. But it is not impossible. According to

Daniel Ingram, whose book gave me an understanding of the technical side of meditation, it is no more difficult than graduating from a university. And for this, it is not necessary to go to live in a monastery. If you meditate an hour a day and receive personal recommendations from an experienced teacher, I think it can take from several months to several years without interruption from your usual life. If you are interested, try to find such a teacher.

Meditation has a hugely positive effect on my life. I believe that the further you go, the more you will understand what I mean. Good luck!

Chapter 24: Pineal Gland Activation and Chakras

Activation of the Pineal Gland Through Guided Meditation (10-15 Minutes)

The pineal gland is the physical location of the Ajna chakra.

This small pine shaped gland is placed in the middle of the brain.

It controls your sleep cycle, sexual maturation, and many other vital hormones. It produces the DMT, the brain's natural psychedelic drug. It helps us in connecting with our spirituality.

Stimulating this small gland will help you in awakening you spiritually. It will help you in interacting with your divine energies. It will help you in seeing through life.

Start with the breathing exercise.

Inhale slowly, take the fresh air deep into your gut. Gather your worries, tensions, and thoughts. Now exhale slowly. Release all your worries and tension with the air.

Clear your mind. Racing thoughts are a distraction. You need peace and calm. Soothe your senses. Clear your mind.

Once again, inhale slowly, take the fresh air deep into your gut. Gather your worries, tensions, and thoughts. Now exhale slowly. Release all your worries and tension with the air.

Clear the waste from your mind. Nothing is important at this very moment. You are the prime source of energy. You are embarking on a journey to enlightenment. Start with peace of mind. Tranquility must prevail everywhere.

One more time, inhale slowly, take the fresh air deep into your gut. Gather your worries, tensions, and thoughts. Now exhale slowly. Release all your worries and tension with the air.

Close your eyes and focus.

Focus on the center of your brain. The pineal gland is located here. Establish contact with it. Let it know that you want to connect.

It is very powerful. It is the source of immense power. It is the seat of the soul. The place of the Ajna chakra.

It has spiritual powers. It will help in your unification with the universe. You will become a part of the great network. You do not need an external source. You are the source.

Breathe into the pineal gland. Fill it with divine power. Energize it. You can charge and activate it.

You will feel some throbbing sensation. It is the pineal gland activating.

Focus on it. Let it know that you want to connect with it. You want to become one with your greater self. The eternal light inside you.

Breathe deeply. You want to amalgamate with this divine light. You want to become one with it. Leave all the negative energies behind. Move towards the source of pure and pious energy. The unblemished aura.

It will fill you. It will enlighten you. It will awaken you. Seek and you will find.

Expunge the pollution out of your system. You will not carry anything this point forward. There is no place for worldly feelings. Love, hate, and animosities become meaningless. They create Karma. You are a forgiving soul.

Move ahead. As one with the power. Focus deep. Breathe Deeper.

It is a long journey. Keep moving.

You will feel immense calm. Light all around you. It isn't hot. It is soothing. This is the light of the soul. Your soul is emanating radiance. Absorb it. It is all for you. Relish it.

Enjoy the moment. It is blissful. It is the moment. You have always desired it.

Now, take a deep breath. Inhale slowly, take the fresh air deep into your gut. Wait for a few moments. Now exhale slowly.

Again, take a deep breath. Inhale slowly, take the fresh air deep into your gut. Wait for a few moments. Exhale.

Rub your palms vigorously. Make them warm. Cover your eyes with them. Keep them covered for a moment.

Now open your eyes very slowly. Do not rush. Loosen your body. Do not get up immediately.

Ponder over your achievements in the process.

CPSIA information can be obtained
at www.ICGtesting.com
Printed in the USA
BVHW091414290621
610728BV00004B/961